# Timeless Tablets

Books by Simon Glustrom

**Timeless Tablets**

**I Would Do It Again — Perhaps**
**A Rabbi's Memoir**

**The Myth and Reality of Judaism**

**The Language of Judaism**

**Living With Your Teenager**

**When Your Child Asks**

# Timeless Tablets

Why the Ten Commandments Still Speak to Us

Rabbi Simon Glustrom

Schreiber Publishing
Rockville, Maryland

# Timeless Tablets
Simon Glustrom

Published by:

## Schreiber Publishing
Post Office Box 4193
Rockville, MD 20849 USA
www.schreiberpublishing.com

**Library of Congress Cataloging-in-Publication Data**

Glustrom, Simon.
  Timeless tablets : why the Ten Commandments still speak to us / Simon Glustrom.
    p. cm.
  ISBN 0-88400-326-4 (pbk.)
  1.  Ten commandments.  2.  Jewish ethics.  I. Title.

BM520.75.G58 2006
296.3'6—dc22

                                        2006018573

**Printed in the United States of America**

I dedicate this book to the people, known
and unknown to me, who are
constantly struggling
to observe the
Ten Commandments

# Acknowledgements

In discussing the eighth commandment, prohibiting stealing, I have included some thoughts on the "plague of plagiarism" among a number of contemporary authors and scholars. I must confess that I have borrowed a great deal of material from ancient, medieval and modem sources. Yet, I have attempted to provide the reader with sources wherever possible. Occasionally I could not remember or find the source to a passage, but I did not consciously conceal a source to sound original.

I have heavily relied on the generous help of several colleagues and friends who read the pages of this manuscript. They did not hesitate to offer me their candid criticism and their encouragement. I accepted both with profound gratitude. These readers shared with me much of their valuable time and talents:

Although we disagreed on several ideological issues, Lippman Bodoff came through with his brilliant editorial skills and his extensive Jewish background. Rabbi Bernard Zlotowitz, an experienced author and noted scholar, patiently worked with me over bagels and coffee. His written and oral suggestions proved invaluable. Professor Leonard Kravitz made many constructive comments based on his vast knowledge of Jewish philosophy and theology. Rabbi Joseph Rudavsky, who served for many years in the rabbinate, did not hesitate to let me know where he agreed and differed with my views, especially in the area of theology. His marginal notes were consistently helpful and challenging.

Rabbi Eugene Korn, whom I met at the tennis club, was a real find. I am fortunate that he agreed to read the manuscript. His sharp eye for finding the right word or expression and his extensive knowledge of classical sources prompted me to question some of my previously held views and opinions. Rabbi David Feldman was especially helpful in discussing with me some of the sensitive issues found in my expanded treatment of the sixth commandment—"You shall not murder." My walking partner, Dr. Sam Menahem, who listened intently as we walked around the track, contributed a number of psychological insights and refreshingly uncommon views on religion and spirituality.

My publisher, Rabbi Mordecai Schreiber, has given me the encouragement that an author looks for after submitting a manuscript. I am most grateful to him for being so supportive and receptive to my suggestions.

I am indebted to Jeffrey Zonenshine who taught me to get started on the word processor. I could always call on Jeffrey for his technical expertise, especially when I had reached an impasse. Several years ago I wrote that without Jeffrey's encouragement I would still be using an unreliable pen and frantically searching for a clean eraser. Marcia Minuskin, Jeffrey's wife, also helped me overcome some of my computer woes.

I can't thank enough my dear wife and life's partner Helen for exploring with me some of the moral problems and dilemmas that I have attempted to grapple with in these pages. Helen's greatest contribution, however, was expressed in the form of a solemn reminder that I was just another *recipient* of the Ten Commandments.

# Table of Contents

# Introduction

With the recent eruption of violent incidents in the public schools, we have heard strong sentiment advocating that the Ten Commandments be prominently posted in our public institutions as a reminder of our solemn obligations to God and our fellow human beings. Since the Ten Commandments are taken directly from the Bible and generally considered a religious document, we can understand why permission has not been granted by the courts since such a display is considered an infringement of the principle of separation between church and state. However, the issue of displaying the Ten Commandments on government property continues to be contested in the courts with powerful forces ready to defend both sides of the controversy.

What should surprise us is that the Ten Commandments, which, according to the biblical text, were brought down by Moses from Mount Sinai, received less than generous treatment by the rabbinic authorities. We know, for example, from the Mishnah Tamid that during the period of the Second Temple the Priests would assemble at the Chamber of Hewn Stones to conduct their daily service. The service consisted of an affirmation of faith, comprised of the recitation of the Ten Commandments and the three paragraphs of the *Shema*. The inclusion of the Decalogue seemed logical since it contains some of the basic principles of the Jewish faith. Yet, the recitation of the Decalogue became an embarrassment to the rabbis because the sectarians or heretics claimed that only the Ten Commandments were revealed at Mount Sinai, not the rest of the Torah.

In a bold move to refute the heretics, the rabbis in the talmudic era removed the Ten Commandments from the daily affirmation of faith (B.Ber. 12a). But in spite of this rabbinic decision, the Ten Commandments continued to be included in the daily service in some isolated communities for many centuries. For example, in the Palestinian synagogue of Old Cairo the inclusion of the Ten Commandments in the daily service continued into the thirteenth century.

The authorities responsible for the exclusion of the Decalogue from the daily liturgy must have encountered vigorous opposition from some of their colleagues. The rabbis go to great lengths to show that the essence of the Ten Commandments is embedded in the *Shema* section, so nothing is really lost by removing the Ten Commandments from the liturgy. Also, as if to compensate for the omission, it became customary for the congregation to stand on the three occasions during the year when the Decalogue was publicly read: in the books of Exodus and Deuteronomy, and on the festival of Shavuot, which commemorates the giving of the Torah.

In spite of the apologetic moves to restore some of the prominence to the Decalogue, it is difficult to understand why it was consigned to a section of some prayerbooks that the worshiper will discover only by accident, at the end of the morning service, where optional readings were placed together as something apart from the liturgy—an afterthought. One gets the feeling that the arrangers of such prayerbooks didn't know quite how to handle the Decalogue, so they decided to slip it into an inconspicuous place. Quite a comedown: from the heights of Mount Sinai to near oblivion!

Fortunately, we do not have to contend with the problem of heretics which threatened the Jewish community in the talmudic era. Yet, there is still a huge number of people who proudly claim that their credo consists of the Ten Commandments, which allows them to embrace the high moral principles found in the Hebrew Bible, but without having to accept the obligations of Jewish ritual. Although these people appear to be sincere in adopting the Ten Commandments as their personal code of behavior, I wonder how many are aware of what the Decalogue really requires of them. What does each commandment include and exclude? Do they feel commanded by God or do they pay their respect to these principles only because they were brought up to recite them? How do those who express an aversion to ritual or prayer deal with the thorny fourth commandment, "Remember the Sabbath day and keep it holy?"

My interest in the Decalogue stems from a long-held belief that it is too precious to be read only three times a year in the synagogue. The Decalogue needs to be reinstated, recited at more regular intervals during the year as a solemn reminder of the awesome message found in this moral guide, which was voluntarily accepted by the Israelites at the dawn of their peoplehood. The Decalogue deserves to be taken off the shelf; it needs to be studied and discussed in the classroom and in the home with the hope that its powerful directives be implemented in our daily lives.

Although the Ten Commandments were omitted from the daily liturgy—and for a valid reason at the time the decision was made—the rabbis in the talmudic period became deeply involved in the interpretation of these deceptively simple declarations. The rabbinic mind was diligently at work, weaving discussions, stories and legends to illustrate and elucidate each of the commandments. The colorful *midrashim,* some fanciful and far-fetched, others direct as a hammer pounding on a nail, were intent on clarifying the meaning of each word and phrase in the Decalogue. These Sages used whatever "tools" were available to them to impress students of the Torah that what happened at Mount Sinai remained an urgent and relevant message for each succeeding generation. To help the reader appreciate the "rabbinic mind"—a phrase coined by the scholar Max Kadushin—I have included several *midrashim* with each of the Ten Commandments. The logical method of these masters may not be easily understood by the modern reader, especially those who have never tried to wrestle with a talmudic text. The Sages followed their own exotic method of reasoning, acceptable in their time. But the message of their interpretations is clear and understandable.

In the *Reflections* preceding the *Insights From the Sages,* I explore the significance of each commandment with an eye toward applying them to some of our current moral dilemmas. In discussing such problems as capital punishment, abortion, or assisted suicide as they relate to the commandment forbidding murder, I offer my personal views without apology or equivocation.

It would be too simplistic to assert that the Ten Commandments are meant to be a panacea for all that is wrong in the world, that of all mankind's ills would evaporate if everyone just observed these humane laws. I regard these commandments as an invaluable guidepost that we should refer to for constant direction as we confront the complex moral problems of our day. The Ten Commandments represent the *minimal requirements* that are needed to sustain a just and durable society. They do not go so far as to require that we love God; they do not obligate us to love our neighbor or the stranger in our midst. Our duty to love others, including God, is found elsewhere in the Torah, but not in the Decalogue. The bar is deliberately set at a realistic level so that it is not beyond the reach of anyone who is able to grasp the meaning of the commandments and willing to abide by them.

New books and articles on the Ten Commandments appear with regularity. It is apparent that the keen interest in this ancient text continues to fascinate scholars and students, both the religious and secular elements of the community. We should warmly welcome these additional contributions to the staggering number of volumes which have already appeared on the Decalogue. Such intense interest on the subject appears to be a clear indication that an ever increasing number of people are seeking ways to renew their ties to the unprecedented event of Revelation that changed the course of history.

אָנֹכִי יְהֹוָה אֱלֹהֶיךָ
אֲשֶׁר הוֹצֵאתִיךָ
מֵאֶרֶץ מִצְרַיִם
מִבֵּית עֲבָדִים.

I am the Lord your God
who brought you out of
the land of Egypt, the
house of bondage.

# First Commandment

# Reflections

What audacity for Moses the Lawgiver to expect, or to be more precise, to demand belief in an invisible God from an oppressed band of former slaves! How could the long-suffering Israelites, steeped in magic and superstition for so many years, suddenly be warned that they were henceforth strictly forbidden to believe in the divinity of an animal or a river or a human being? They were charged by Moses to renounce what they had long regarded as sacred or divine and begin to place their faith in a mysterious Being demanding that they practice a body of laws that they had never heard of before their encounter at Mount Sinai. Moses' unprecedented call for faith in one God was interrupted by the episode of the Golden Calf, but eventually, after this and other lapses by the Israelites, the belief in ethical monotheism took hold and was eventually accepted by some of the world's major religions.

Before delving into the essence of the Ten Commandments and their application to our daily lives, we should attempt to understand what the concept of commandment conveys to us. Should a biblical commandment be compared to an order handed down by the military or the local police authorities that carries the threat of punishment if we refuse to comply? Some of the commandments in the Decalogue, if ignored or deliberately violated, do not carry a penalty in a court of law. Refusal to follow them is a matter between the individual and one's conscience or the individual and God. Even the divine retribution for violating most of the commandments is not clearly spelled out in the Bible.

The religiously committed person is willing to accept the idea of being commanded by God because he/she acknowledges that the need to follow moral principles is essential if we are to maintain a viable society. Anything less than a commandment would be understood as a lukewarm suggestion, a practical piece of advice, but nothing more. The believer acknowledges that the commandments found in the Decalogue express the will of God and are affixed with the divine signature.

The first commandment is set apart from the other nine because it does not sound like a commandment, and can be easily misunderstood as an opening statement or a preface. In fact, a number of Christian versions of the Ten Commandments commence with the following verse, "You shall have no other gods before Me." The first commandment deals exclusively with accepting faith in God as an underlying principle that gives legitimacy to the other commandments, elevating them to a sacred status.

The Hebrew Bible does not usually dwell on the need to believe in God. Faith in God's existence is taken for granted throughout the Bible. The psalmist confirms this view when he declares that "the fool says in his heart there is no God." In Jewish thought, greater emphasis is placed on trust and reliance upon God—*bitahon* in Hebrew—rather than the charge to have faith in God's existence. The message of the first commandment is unique in biblical thought. Not until the medieval period in Jewish history did the philosophers dwell on the importance of faith and how it was to be understood.

But one may ask why is it necessary to introduce the Decalogue with the charge to believe in God *before* introducing the other commandments? Isn't it possible to accept the value of the other commandments without assuming the burden of faith? The question is not new. For years religious skeptics have firmly declared that they, and others whom they respected, were highly ethical and law-abiding people although they were not comfortable believing in a God whose existence was difficult to imagine.

These skeptics claim to make moral decisions with regularity but without the need to be commanded by a higher authority in order to do the right thing. They are convinced that making a moral choice, such as refraining from adultery or theft, is the safest and most reasonable path to follow. In the long run, it simply pays to act honorably. Or they deliberately choose to take the moral route because they have learned from personal experience that they would be treated with the same respect with which they treat others in business or in their social relationships. Or they have long ago decided to take the high road because they just don't want to struggle with a troubled conscience at the end of the day.

These reasons for choosing to make moral decisions on one's own without the need for divine interference in their lives cannot be easily dismissed. Most of us have come in contact with agnostics or secularists who are uncompromising moralists. They would never choose to cheat a customer or deceive an employee.

Yet, if we are truly candid, we will admit that many of us choose to make moral decisions only when it is convenient to do so, requiring little effort on our part. The need to rationalize our moral lapses is stronger than most of us are willing to recognize. But when we accept the premise that we are commanded by God to follow a difficult or critical moral decision, we cannot comfortably rationalize our need to do otherwise. When confronted with a divine commandment to honor a parent or to refrain from giving false testimony in a courtroom, we will not readily compromise with the gravity of a religious commandment that is too sacred to ignore.

Some commandments run contrary to our basic desires, such as the prohibition against adultery or covetousness. One of the functions of accepting a moral code ordained by God is to help us keep our instincts in check, to put the brake on our raw impulses. If taken seriously, a commandment does not leave us with the option to defy or to delay an urgent call to moral action even if it appears unpopular with the masses.

Accepting the commandments before understanding them fully entails a crucial risk. But that is precisely what the ancient Israelites chose to do when they stood at the foot of Mount Sinai and solemnly declared: "We will do and we will hear (*na-aseh v'nishma*)," or more precisely, "We will do and we will understand." The Israelites were not signing a business contract that requires prior understanding of the terms of the agreement. They agreed in the covenant at Sinai to obligate themselves to God's higher authority although they did not yet fully grasp what they were agreeing to in advance. The performance of the commandments would lead to an eventual understanding of what these principles of conduct really meant.

The Israelites who stood at Sinai did not have a problem with belief vs. non-belief in a deity. Their problem primarily was that they had difficulty believing in an invisible God. What was needed in this critical juncture in their history required a leap of faith, their acceptance of the thought that this protective God would not reveal everything about Himself to the Israelites, even to their leader Moses. For every generation God's essence would remain enshrouded in mystery.

To this very day the same leap of faith remains at the heart of religious commitment. God's essence is no less a mystery to us than He was to Abraham or to Moses. But what do we mean when we speak of faith in God as a mystery? What the believer can know or learn about God is infinitesimal, compared to what lies beyond his/her comprehension. We moderns may know more than the ancients about what God is not, yet, God's true essence continues to elude our understanding. This cloud of mystery associated with God will forever confound us. But without the acceptance of mystery, belief in the existence of God and the attraction of religion is difficult to sustain, especially when we see how the wicked prosper and the good suffer so often in history. Any attempt to completely de-mystify and humanize God reduces the power of religion to the prosaic thought that God was created in the image of man.

What is not generally understood by skeptics is that acceptance of God's commandments is not a call for surrender of our freedom. We are not asked to renounce our free will or to compromise our rational faculties. Our acceptance of the divine commandments does not imply silent surrender to God's orders. Even the devout are entitled to express occasional doubt. They have the right, even the obligation to exercise their "justice muscle" and question God.

Abraham Joshua Heschel, in his brilliant analysis of the Hasidic master Reb Menahem Mendl of Kotzk, attributes this insight to the Rebbe: "A man who lived by honesty could not be expected to suppress his anxiety when tormented by profound perplexity. He had to speak out audaciously. Man should never capitulate, even to the Lord" (*A Passion for Truth*, p. 269).

Judaism, along with other religious groups, asks for some degree of submission to a higher power, an acceptance on our part that man is not the measure of all things. Although we are encouraged to express our rational opinions and to challenge previous theories, we are not capable of grasping the sum total of all truth by virtue of our limited powers of understanding.

Acceptance of the commandments implies a willingness to follow certain moral rules and regulations that may not necessarily seem palatable or fashionable to us at a particular stage of our lives, but have nevertheless withstood the test of time. Since the commandments express God's will, they are worthy of our acceptance even if they are often inconvenient or require personal sacrifice to abide by these standards of behavior.

Whether we are happy with the thought or not, all law-abiding citizens are expected to yield to the authority of the state or municipality in which we live. We cannot drive as fast as we would like; we cannot leave our property in disrepair. If we choose to remain lawful citizens we cannot cavalierly follow our personal preferences. Thus, the need to acknowledge a higher authority is by no means confined to the area of religion.

Today we continue to debate the question whether the "Ten Utterances," as the Ten Commandments are called in the Bible, are absolute demands imposed by God or rather valuable directives that are subject to critical evaluation, even revision when necessary. Are there extenuating circumstances when the commandments may be modified or enhanced in order to attain an even higher good than is found in the biblical text?

The lofty commandments found in the Decalogue are not all absolute. How are we expected to honor a sexually abusive parent? How can we observe the Sabbath day by refraining from work if the seventh day is the only day we can find work and our dependents are in dire need of basic necessities, food or clothing. No one would expect an observant Jew to interpret the commandment to remember the Sabbath day or to honor one's parents so literally that he would be physically or emotionally harmed by insisting on observing the law at all cost. Certainly there are times when a specific commandment must be set aside in order to save a life—our own or that of another person. And even when a person is not critically ill, food may be prepared on the Sabbath to provide nourishment for an ailing patient.

Although the commandments are not absolute, neither are they arbitrary. They were not proclaimed just to test our loyalty to God or to our religious tradition. The commandments continue to remain viable even as they were throughout the centuries. They have been honored, in theory at least, by most civilized societies. The Ten Commandments may be regarded as the minimal requirements for achieving and sustaining a moral society.

The Decalogue opens with the word *anokhi,* meaning "I" in both versions found in Exodus (chapter 20) and Deuteronomy (chapter 5). In the second version the Decalogue is preceded by a verse proclaimed by Moses to the people of Israel: *Anokhi omed bein Adonai u'vein-eikhem,* "I stood between God and you." The insightful Hasidic master Menahem Mendl of Kotzk. deliberately misread the verse to teach a profound lesson: It is the *anokhi,* the "I" or ego that stands between God and you.

Could this be the compelling reason why the first commandment, the preamble to the Decalogue is met with resistance? The protest may sound something like this: *I* don't need to be directed by a higher authority to be told what is good for *me* or for the members of *my* family. *I* may or may not choose to accept the directives found in the Decalogue, but if *I* do, it is because *I* alone have come to the conclusion that the words meet with *my* own approval. *I* must reserve the right to decide if *I* am to remain a free and independent person.

Very few Jewish thinkers would go so far as to accept the view that the human ego itself is destructive and thus, one should passively submit to the Divine Ego; such a false notion is tantamount to the claim that when we express personal needs and desires we become estranged from God. Many of our prayers found in our liturgy deal with our personal needs. Menahem Mendl sought to avoid a clash between the Divine Ego (*anokhi*) and the human ego. On the one hand, he railed against the overbearing human ego—selfishness and self-centeredness—but on the other hand, he battled against complete submission or surrender to God's demands of us.

The Hebrew language contains two words to express the first person singular: *ani* and *anokhi*. *Anokhi* usually refers to God. *Ani* may refer to either God or man. The Ten commandments are introduced by the word *anokhi* rather than *ani* in order to send a clear message that the ground rules should be established from the outset. The boundaries between God and man are clear and unmistakable. God cannot become a mortal human being just as a human cannot replace God. When we imagine that God can assume human characteristics and become "like one of us," then God is no longer unique. The divine mystique is shattered. We presume to understand God's "mind" and how God operates in the world, very much like other humans. Moreover, when humans regard themselves as divine, they may claim themselves to be omniscient and infallible, just as god-kings have attempted to do throughout the ages.

This need to set up boundaries is found in the book of Exodus in anticipation of the Revelation at Mount Sinai: "And the Lord said to Moses, You shall set bounds for the people round about, saying, `Beware of going up the mountain or touching the border of it. . .'"(Exodus 19:10-12).

Perhaps now we can understand why the second commandment forbidding all forms of idolatry is a necessary sequel to the opening commandment. Where there is no clear boundary between God and man—*anokhi* and *ani*—idolatry becomes a major problem, despite the absence of visible idols in our midst.

"I am the Lord your God who brought you out of the land of Egypt, out of the house of bondage." The renowned medieval Jewish philosopher and poet Judah Halevi questioned why the opening words of the Decalogue recorded in the Book of Exodus do not refer to God's role as Creator of the universe or of the human race, certainly a more miraculous feat than bringing a downtrodden people out of slavery. (It should be noted that further on, the Sabbath commandment *does* refer to God as Creator of world.) The Israelites who stood at Sinai were able to relate to the Exodus because they experienced it first hand. The miracle of creation was too abstruse and remote to make an impression on these former slaves.

Another reason for associating God with the Exodus instead of the miracle of creation was to draw a distinction between God and the world that He brought into being. God and nature are not one and the same. They should not be confused. To be sure, we have reason to stand in awe before the majesty of nature, but we do not worship God's creation—only the Creator, and not that which was created. The distinguished historian Salo Baron emphasized this principle of Judaism in his *Social and Religious History of the Jews*: "Little wonder that again and again the Bible draws a sharp distinction between the nations who worship nature in some form or other and the Jewish people whose chief concern is its central position in history." (Vol. I, p. 15)

The Book of Deuteronomy is explicit on the question of the God of history as opposed to the God of nature. "And when you look up to the sky and behold the sun and the moon and the stars, the whole heavenly host, you must not be lured into bowing down to them or serving them. These the Lord your God allotted to other peoples everywhere under heaven; but you the Lord took and brought out of Egypt, that iron blast furnace, to be His very own people, as is now the case" (4:19 20).

But why must the Creator remain distinct from His creation? Why does normative Judaism reject the attractive doctrine of pantheism that identifies God with everything in the universe? Why not accept the intriguing idea that God and nature are one and the same? Didn't the brilliant philosopher Spinoza identify God with nature? Didn't Einstein as well associate God with the majestic world of nature?

Although we have much to learn about the infinite complexity of the natural world, nature by and large is cyclical and usually predictable. We know exactly when the moon will wax and wane; we can track the path and positions of the moon as it travels around the sun; we know precisely when a solar eclipse will take place. God, on the other hand, does not follow a predictable pattern, at least not one known to humankind. We do not comprehend nor will we ever grasp all there is to know about God's actions and reactions.

Moreover, the world of nature does not always react or respond to an individual's behavior. The sun continued to rise in the morning even during the darkest days of the Holocaust. The stars didn't show dismay or anger when Stalin annihilated millions of his own people. On September 11th, 2001, when a part of Lower Manhattan was obliterated by fiendish aggressors, the natural warmth and beauty of the summer day was not affected throughout most of the country. Yet, even if God will not or possibly cannot prevent acts of brutality, nevertheless, God "mourns" along with the victims of brutality. God is not dispassionate or indifferent to the plight of the downtrodden in each generation.

Nature cannot literally request anything of human beings, unless we are speaking metaphorically. A snow-capped mountain or a lush rain forest is not concerned whether we fulfill our human potential. Offering us moral guidance is not the business of the world of nature. However, people of faith fervently believe that choosing ethical priorities in life is of supreme importance to God. True, a sunrise or sunset can inspire a sense of humility and awe, but neither phenomenon can urge us to arrive at a moral decision or treat our neighbor with kindness.

A person of Jewish faith who is acquainted with the history of his or her people can comfortably identify with the recitation of the first commandment, "I am the Lord your God who brought you forth from the land of Egypt, out of the house of bondage." But how does the non-Jew relate to this particular command? If the Decalogue represents the minimal requirement for all people who seek to live by a moral code, what does the Exodus mean to them? The Exodus has served as an inspirational event, a paradigm that changed the course of history, a call to freedom for the persecuted and the disenfranchised over many centuries. The Pilgrims who came to these shores seeking political and religious asylum from the oppressive monarchy in England were inspired by the flight of the Israelites. They were confident that God would protect them from their contemporary Pharaoh just as God watched over the ancient Israelites.

The black slaves who were brought to these shores in shackles also found their solace in the Exodus story. The Israelite flight to freedom with Moses at their side and God in command comprised their freedom song. How many of their spirituals expressing travail, faith and hope were based on the Exodus theme! And in our time as well the struggle for civil rights was closely identified with the Israelite struggle. Martin Luther King crafted some of his most moving sermons and speeches, using the biblical theme of the Exodus as his master text. His brothers and sisters could personally relate to the Exodus as their source of religious inspiration; King also hoped to appeal to the hardened hearts of those southern whites who were immersed in the Old Testament, and yet, were loathe to apply the text to the shameful predicament of the blacks in their segregated communities.

One of the main passages in the Haggadah which is read at the Passover Seder contains the prescription: "In each generation, every individual should feel as if he or she had actually been redeemed from Mitzrayim." (Translation found in the Rabbinical Assembly Haggadah, p.67). The text emphasizes that *everyone*, not only direct descendants of the Israelites at Sinai, is asked to look upon the Exodus as the script of an inclusive human drama, not merely the record of some remote and unrelated event that has meaning for a single people.

# Insights from the Sages

## God speaks with the Israelites in their own tongue

When the Holy One came to present the Torah to Israel, He spoke to them in a language they knew and understood.

"I (*anokhi*) am the Lord your God" (Ex. 20:2). R. Nehemiah asked: What kind of word is *anokhi*? It is an Egyptian word. . . How may God's need to use an Egyptian word for "I" be explained? By the story of a mortal king whose son had been captured. The son spent a long period among his captors and learned their language. Finally the king took revenge on his enemies and brought back his son. But when he tried to talk with him in his own language, the son did not understand. What did the king do? He began to speak with him in the language of his captors. The Holy One had to do the same with Israel. During all the years Israel spent in Egypt, they learned the Egyptian speech. Finally, when the Holy One redeemed them and came to give them the Torah, they couldn't understand it. So the Holy One said: I will speak to them in Egyptian. Thus, the Holy One inaugurated the giving of the Torah by using the word *anokhi*, a form of the Egyptian *anokh*.

(Tanhuma B.Yitro 16)

## God Must First Convince Israel

Why were the Ten Commandments not stated at the beginning of the Torah? A parable: To what may this be compared? A king who entered a province said to the people: May I be your monarch? The people answered: Have you done anything for us that you should be ruler over us? What did he do then? He built a city wall for them; he brought in the water supply, and he fought their battles. Then he asked them: May I be your king? They responded: Yes, yes. Likewise God. He brought the Israelites out of Egypt, divided the Sea for them, sent down the manna for them, brought up the well and produced the quails for them. He fought for them the battle against Amalek. Then God said to them: I will be your King, and they responded: Yes, yes.

(Mekhilta Bahodesh Ch. 5)

## Everyone Has Access to the Torah

Why was the Torah not given in the Land of Israel? In order that the nations of the world should not have an excuse for saying: Because it was given in Israel's land, therefore, we have not accepted it. Another reason: To avoid dissension among the tribes. Otherwise, one might have claimed: The Torah was given in my territory. And the other might have claimed: The Torah was given in my territory. Therefore, the Torah was given in the desert, publicly and openly in a place belonging to no one. The Torah is compared to three things: to the desert, to fire, and to water. This is to tell you that just as these three things are free to all who come into the world, so are the words of Torah free to all who come into the world.

(Mekhilta Bahodesh Ch. 5)

לֹא יִהְיֶה לְךָ אֱלֹהִים אֲחֵרִים עַל פָּנָי.
לֹא תַעֲשֶׂה לְךָ פֶסֶל וְכָל תְּמוּנָה אֲשֶׁר
בַּשָּׁמַיִם מִמַּעַל וַאֲשֶׁר בָּאָרֶץ מִתַּחַת
וַאֲשֶׁר בַּמַּיִם מִתַּחַת לָאָרֶץ.
לֹא תִשְׁתַּחֲוֶה לָהֶם וְלֹא תָעָבְדֵם כִּי
אָנֹכִי יְהֹוָה אֱלֹהֶיךָ אֵל קַנָּא פֹּקֵד
עֲוֹן אָבֹת עַל בָּנִים עַל שִׁלֵּשִׁים
וְעַל רִבֵּעִים לְשֹׂנְאָי. וְעֹשֶׂה חֶסֶד
לַאֲלָפִים לְאֹהֲבַי וּלְשֹׁמְרֵי מִצְוֹתָי.

You shall not have other gods besides me.
You shall not make for yourself a sculptured image
or any likenss of what is in the heaven above
or on the earth below, or in the waters under the
earth. You shall not bow down to them or serve
them. For I the Lord your God am an impassioned
God, visiting the guilt of the parents upon their
children, upon the third and upon the fourth
generation of those who reject Me, but showing
kindness to the thousandth generation of those
who love Me and keep My commandments.

# Second Commandment

# Reflections

Why is idolatry given such a bad press in the Hebrew Bible? Why is the Torah unalterably opposed to worshiping other deities in addition to the God of Israel? All idolaters were not necessarily evil men. Terah, for example, the father of Abraham and, according to a well-known Midrash, a seller of idols, must have exerted some positive influence on his son who would become the founder of a great monotheistic religion. Though perhaps naive and misguided, Terah must have done something right to have helped raise such an imaginative and strong-willed child. Jethro, as well, a Midianite priest and father-in-law of Moses, was probably a worshiper of alien gods although he showed reverence for the God of Israel, at least originally, after he heard what God had done for the Israelites. Indeed, an entire Sabbath Torah reading is named after Jethro! Jethro turned out to become a great moral force who, we are told, mentored Moses and strongly influenced him.

Is it not then possible to have faith in a physical god and still remain a good person? Is the worship of a visible or tactile god not preferable to a repudiation of religion altogether? The Hebrew Bible takes an uncompromising view on this issue: You cannot be loyal to God and tolerate the worship of any other gods; all of them are false and must be repudiated. The two forms of worship are mutually exclusive.

One would think that the Israelites could have gracefully accepted the recognition of other gods. Didn't the ancient Greeks tolerate many gods in their pantheon? Could it have been an inordinate fear that if the Israelites were given choices, they would have preferred a more permissive, a less demanding god than the uncompromising God of Israel?

The answer is obviously yes! However, the function of a mature religion is not meant merely to provide its adherents with a comfortable feeling. They cannot freely choose a divinity who reflects their current mood or impulsive wishes. Such "hunting and pecking" is comparable to the child who, when refused a request by one parent, goes to the second parent, hoping for a more favorable response. The prophet Elijah forcefully put the question to his people when he asked them outright: "How long will you halt between two opinions?" Elijah wanted to impress upon his fickle brethren that they had to choose between the one true God or a counterfeit deity. They could not have it both ways and still remain faithful to the one true God.

The older more traditional translations of the second commandment spoke of a "jealous God" who would not tolerate allegiance to any other divinity. The new Jewish Publication Society translation tones down the all-too-human description of God's reaction to idolatry. It reads: "For I the Lord your God am an impassioned God." Both translations convey the same feeling, that God cannot remain passive or indifferent to idolatry or polytheism. God is passionately reactive when an individual or a community goes astray.

Normally we are advised to advocate a spirit of accommodation and tolerance in our daily affairs. We need to show understanding for the different forms of belief, the rich variety of religious practices in many of our communities, if we are to preserve a humane society. Yet, the sense of the second commandment clearly conveys that God will not tolerate those who wish to accommodate themselves to other gods that are visible and attractive to the eye, but without lasting value or substance. The price of compromise with idolatry is too high. If there are many gods one may choose to worship, then, by definition, there are many conflicting moral codes that may be chosen. When people feel free to choose a god based on the principles that seem most popular or convenient at the time, then there is no reason to maintain a deep and abiding relationship with a God who sets one set—and not many sets—of moral standards and requirements for us to follow.

But why the need to believe exclusively in a deity that appears so remote, so elusive? Why the need for such a sophisticated faith in an invisible God? If passion is an essential ingredient in religion, don't we sacrifice some of this exhilaration when we are required to put our faith in a God who cannot be seen, touched or defined? We remember how the Israelites became so ecstatic in the presence of the golden calf. The reason was obvious: They could dance without restraint in the presence of a visible deity that they helped to create with their contributions of gold. They did not have to imagine what their molten god looked like. They were satisfying a basic, primitive need. To place one's belief in an abstraction requires greater effort and challenge. Only by stretching the mind and imagination can one begin to grasp the mystique surrounding God. Once the veil of mystery is removed, then a deity becomes quantified like any other object; he becomes subject to decay and death, and no longer the Creator and Master of life and death. Such a deity is reduced to a familiar object that we can describe and comprehend. Once God can be understood and defined, we lose the essential value of placing our faith in an infinite being.

"Visiting the guilt of the fathers upon the children, upon the third and upon the fourth generations of those who reject Me." There are few passages in the entire Torah which have incited more critical reaction than this enigmatic verse. Religious skeptics, however, take the view that the God of Israel depicted in the second commandment appears harsh and unjust. Why should innocent children be made to suffer for the sins of their fathers? Granted that the offspring are frequently known to suffer from the decadent influence of sinful parents or grandparents. But what does God have against the blameless, the innocent children who cannot choose their parents or grand-parents?

The view that children should be made to suffer for the sins of their elders did not go unchallenged by later generations. The Book of Deuteronomy, which is believed by many students of the Bible to have been written much later than the Book of Exodus, expresses a more moderate view: "Parents shall not be put to death for children, nor children be put to death for parents: A person shall be put to death for his own crime" (Deut. 24:16). We cannot be certain that this verse emphasizing individual responsibility was meant as a direct refutation of the second commandment. If so, why then is the second commandment repeated without any amendment in the fifth chapter of Deuteronomy? Other changes *are* found in the second version of the Decalogue.

Two major prophets as well challenged the theory of extended punishment to future generations found in the second commandment. The Prophet Jeremiah exclaims, "In those days, they shall no longer say, 'Parents have eaten sour grapes and children's teeth are blunted.' But everyone shall die for his own sins: Whosoever eats sour grapes, his teeth shall be blunted" (Jeremiah 31: 29-30).

The Prophet Ezekiel also questioned divine retribution of innocent offspring: "As I live—declares the Lord God—this proverb shall no longer be current among you in Israel. . .The person who sins, only he shall die"(18: 1-4).

It is obvious that both major prophets were critical of the harsh view of vicarious punishment expressed in the Decalogue. They called for its reversion. We cannot be certain, however, whether they wanted to see the old doctrine replaced in the remote future or in their own generation. The talmudic Sages expressed the view that the doctrine of individual responsibility came into effect from the time of Ezekiel, not in the far-off future (B. Makkot 24a). The powerful words uttered by Ezekiel carried sufficient weight to replace the old theology with a more humane doctrine based on personal responsibility.

The medieval commentator Abraham ibn Ezra also sought

to resolve the dilemma. He observed that the Hebrew word *po-ked* used in the second commandment does not connote punishment but rather memory and remembrance. Thus, God remembers the sins of the ancestors unto future generations, but God does not punish them for He anticipates their repentance. This is ibn Ezra's way of preserving God's sense of justice and fairness without having to alter the sacred text.

The highly regarded authority Moses Maimonides (1135-1204), commenting on the second commandment, observes that God "restricts Himself to the fourth generation only because the farthest that a person can see of his offspring is the fourth generation" (*Guide for the Perplexed*, 1-54). Maimonides concludes that the Torah reminds us to be aware that our actions affect all those born during our lifetime. He does not say specifically that God deliberately punishes the blameless offspring of the idolater; what he does imply is that the offspring suffer from his harmful influence so long as he continues to live without repentance. Rather than changing or criticizing the text, he gives it a sociological or scientific meaning based on his personal observation. Maimonides masterfully saves the text from religious skeptics, which comprises the central theme of his monumental book.

Why does the contemporary student of religion question the premise of the second commandment? The author of our biblical text attributed all disease, sickness or premature death to human sinfulness. Without question there had to be cause and effect for everything. God rewarded the righteous and punished the wicked. The sons of Aaron were consumed by fire because they must have performed a reprehensible act in the sanctuary, although we are not told what their sin was other than lighting a "foreign fire." Miriam became leprous because she spoke ill of her brother Moses. Misfortune did not just occur because of accidental circumstance or a situation beyond one's control. Since God was the Creator of both good *and* evil, He would mete out reward and punishment as was befitting a controlling power over man's destiny.

We need not place the blame on God or question His influence in our lives when we observe that children brought up by moral parents occasionally become victims of intolerable suffering and even premature death. Their misfortune need not be attributed to divine retribution upon the family but possibly to a genetic flaw or unexplainable circumstances. Rather than attribute the child's misfortune to a chastising God whose wrath must be avoided, they should be able to look to God as a supporter who suffers along with anxious parents and grandparents. God is on their side, "in their corner." Who, if not God, accepts their prayers for the restoration of the child's health? Whether this same compassionate God has the power to reverse the course of a devastating disease or a terminal illness depends on our expectation of God's powers.

*"But showing kindness to the thousandth generation of those that love Me and keep My commandments."* How does one show love for God? It is obvious from the biblical verses in Deuteronomy that faithfully following God's moral requirements is the way to demonstrate our love. Robert Gordis, who taught Bible at the Jewish Theological Seminary, once remarked that the way we convey love for God in the Hebrew language is no different than the way we express love for another human being. Unlike Christian theologians who often cite two Greek word-concepts to differentiate between spiritual and carnal love—agape vs. eros—only one expression in Hebrew (*ahavah*) expresses all forms of love: the love of a human being for God, the love of one person for another, and the love between man and woman.

Professor Gordis's insight should help us further understand what love of God may mean, based on our capacity to love another human. We show our love for God when we place our trust in Him without setting up conditions. Furthermore, we strengthen that love when we refuse to ask God to show us signs as proof of His love for us. And contrary to the aphorism that was once quoted so widely, love for another person or for God *does* mean having to say, "I'm sorry!"

The expression, "to love God," is not found at all in the first four books of the Torah. However, in Deuteronomy it is mentioned several times, including the *Shema*, which was incorporated into the prayer book: "And you shall love the Lord your

God with all your heart, with all your soul and with all your might."

Some people are under the mistaken impressions that love for God entails a union of the soul with the Creator, which the mystics call *unio mystica.* Gershom Scholem, the outstanding authority on Jewish mysticism, reminded us that even the Spanish Kabbalists who placed great value on *devekut*—communion with God—did not negate the independent existence of the soul. Furthermore, Martin Buber, the celebrated theologian who was deeply influenced by Hasidism in his writings, wrote movingly about the "I" in relationship to the "Eternal Thou." The "I" always remains distinct without submerging its individuality.

Why does God continue punishment up to the fourth generation among those who reject Him, while extending kindness to those who love Him for a thousand generations? It seems that a distinction is being made between God's demand for justice and His overwhelming compassion. There is no contest between these two divine attributes.

On another level, however, the verse conveys the idea that evil, as contagious as it may appear, enjoys a short life; it loses its attractiveness after a limited run. Goodness, on the other hand, expressed by loving God, is far more contagious and durable. Most people are attracted to the love of rather than the rejection of God. Idolatry, whether in ancient or modern form, does not continue to command the sustained allegiance and devotion that trust in God can summon within us.

Is idolatry still a problem for modern man? True, idolatry in its ancient form is no longer a threat to seduce modern man, but we may certainly feel compelled to associate idolatry with the worship of success or material things, which continues to plague our generation. And what of the blind attraction that so many people have for sparkling Hollywood personalities who dazzle their fawning public? Rabbi Shmuley Boteach, who had befriended some of the most prominent celebrities in the entertainment world, recently admitted in the Jewish weekly *Forward* that the idolization of celebrities threatens the essence of the Decalogue. Boteach wrote: "If we were to engage in sincere introspection, we would have to admit that all of us who partake of the popular culture have become closet idolaters. And in no area is this truer than in our fixation with the lives of celebrities. . . Our hero worship of those with face and name recognition has gone from a pastime to a devotion; from a recreation to a noxious form of veneration."

Will Herberg, author of *Judaism and Modern Man* defined idolatry in its present form as the "absolutization of the relative." When science, for example, which has much to offer mankind, is held to be the only truth, the ultimate value, then this, says Herberg, becomes a modern form of idolatry. The same can be said about any relative good that may become elevated to an absolute good—race, nation, class, state, ideology or party. These have become some of the dominant idolatries of our time.

It is apparent that almost everyone places his/her total confidence and allegiance in something. If God does not become a supreme value, then another "god" assumes top priority in one's hierarchy of values. If the accumulation of wealth, the golden calf, becomes one's obsession, then the god called "mammon" (lit. money or wealth) rules supreme in place of the eternal God. God is downsized, so to speak, to become merely a relative good.

Some relativists claim that belief in God is understandable if you are naive, superstitious or just unable to summon up your own resources to place your destiny in your own hands. For those who are so dependent that they must learn to "lean on Him," belief in God may be understandable, but for the tough-minded, the self-reliant who depend on their own mental capacity, placing trust in God is unnecessary, in fact, a sign of weakness. Assigning God to a second class berth in one's value system instead of the supreme good becomes another form of idolatry, no less reprehensible than putting one's faith in a molten calf or a grove of trees, which was strictly forbidden by our forebears in ancient times.

Even if we are firmly committed to belief in God, disavowing the relativist position, we still may not expect to convince another person with different experiences to follow our path of belief. Suppose a person has turned away from religious belief due to a disappointing personal experience within his church or synagogue or because faith in a caring God has lost its appeal after learning about the atrocities of the Holocaust. It is patently unfair to judge another person's character based primarily on his acceptance or rejection of religious belief. If we care to engage a skeptical neighbor in religious dialogue, we should maintain the position that the skeptic keep an open and receptive mind. By the same token, by making such a request of the religious skeptic, we too should maintain an openness to listen and to confront challenging views that could possibly affect our own long-held beliefs.

# Insights From The Sages

## God Will Not Destroy What Man Needs to Survive

Our masters taught: Some philosophers asked the Jewish elders in Rome, "If your God has no desire for idolatry, why then does He not have it cease to exist?" The elders replied, "If what was worshiped were something the world had no need of, God would have made it cease to exist. But people worship the sun and the moon, the stars and the planets. Should He, because of fools, make the world cease to exist? So the world must continue to exist. As for fools, who act wrongly—they will have to render an account." Another example: Say a man stole a measure of wheat and continued to sow it in the ground; by right it should not grow, but the world must continue to exist. As for fools, who act wrongly—they will be accountable.

(B. Avodah Zarah 54b)

## Idolatry Weakens God's Influence

"You forgot the God who brought you forth" (Deut. 32:18). Each time I sought to do you good, you weakened the Power on high. You stood by the Red Sea and proclaimed, "This is my God, and I will praise Him" (Ex. 15:2), and then you returned and said, "Let us appoint a captain, and let us return to Egypt" (Num. 14:4). You stood at Sinai and said, "All that the Lord has spoken to us we will do," and I sought to do you good, but you returned and said to the calf, "This is your god, O Israel." Whenever I seek to do you good, you weaken the Power on high.

(Sifre Deuteronomy Ha'azinu 319)

## God Cannot Compromise with Idolatry

What is the proof that a person may not resort to idolatry [even if it promised healing]? If an ailing Jew is advised, "Approach such-and-such an idol and you will be healed," he is forbidden to approach it, for we are told, "He that sacrifices to a god other than the Lord shall be utterly doomed" (Ex. 22:19). Since he who worships other gods is doomed, it is better for him to die of his illness in this world than bring such condemnation upon himself.

Not only is idolatry forbidden to be used in healing the sick, so are all things related to idolatry. For example, if a person is told, "Take some of the incense offered up to the idol or a piece of wood from the idol's grove and make a charm of it, and thereby be healed," he may not take either of these, for Scripture says, "Let nothing that has been doomed stick to your hand"(Deut. 13:18). Why not? Because there is no substance in them; they are of no avail whatsoever, as Scripture says, "Be not afraid of them, for they cannot do evil, neither is it in them to do good" (Jer. 10:5).

(Exodus Rabbah 16:2)

## Moses Defends Israel's Moral Lapse

Moses spoke up: "Master of the universe, this calf would be just right to assist You." The Holy One: "How can he assist Me?" Moses: "You cause the winds to blow, and he may bring down rain; You cause the sun to shine, and he might do the same with the moon; You cause the trees to grow, and he might make the plants to sprout." God: "Like them, even you, Moses, seem to be led astray by the calf!" Moses: " So, the thing isn't much. It eats grass and at the same time may be slaughtered [like other calves]. `Why then should your anger blaze forth against Your people?'" (Ex.32: ll).

(Exodus Rabbah 43:6)

לֹא תִשָּׂא אֶת שֵׁם
יְהֹוָה אֱלֹהֶיךָ לַשָּׁוְא
כִּי לֹא יְנַקֶּה יְהֹוָה
אֵת אֲשֶׁר יִשָּׂא אֶת
שְׁמוֹ לַשָּׁוְא .

You shall not swear falsely
by the name of the Lord
your God; for the Lord
will not clear one who swears
falsely by His name.

# Third Commandment

# Reflections

Many curious students of religion and ethics have pondered over the intent of the third commandment and why it occupies a hallowed place with some of the other major commandments: You shall not murder, commit adultery, steal, etc.

Perhaps we should resort to the process of elimination in order to discover why the Torah included this commandment among the "Big Ten."

Is the third command meant as a warning against the use of obscene language in one's daily speech? It stands to reason that the Jewish tradition, along with other religious disciplines, strongly encourages the use of refined and elegant language. Vile speech not only betrays a sense of restlessness and discontent, often combined with angry feelings; it is also an abuse of the divine gift of human language. Yet, it is highly doubtful whether the Torah is here addressing the problem of failing to control one's daily speech. Almost everyone, regardless of cultural or social background, is capable of expressing a profanity or, at the very least, to feel like uttering a profanity here and there without necessarily verbalizing it. The occasional outburst is not merely an instinctual response under emotional pressure; it may also serve to relieve tension and even prevent a harmful physical response.

There is a great difference between an occasional outburst of inelegant language as a response to frustration or anger, and the use of abusive speech as a substitute for civil discourse. Take, for example, the angry verbal reaction expressed toward a driver who has invaded our parking space. Our verbal outburst directed to the aggressive driver can and often does result in serious consequences. Frequently we read reports about the horrible repercussions originating with verbal assault and ending with a vengeful act by the insulted party.

The Jewish tradition has much to say about the need to develop the habit of clean speech. The concept of *shemirat ha-lashon* (lit. guarding one's tongue) not only applies to the sin of gossip and slander against another person; it admonishes us as well to avoid profanity. Yet, it is apparent that the third commandment is directed at a transgression more serious than the use of indecent or abusive language.

Can the commandment then refer to the all-too-common inclusion of God's name when uttering a profanity—mingling the sacred with the profane? People who are sensitive to the use of appropriate speech are offended when God's revered name is reduced to an expletive. Those who take their faith seriously and use God's name with awe and reverence are especially justified in resenting expressions that degrade the very foundation of their belief.

And yet, it is doubtful that reducing God's name to an expletive is the moral problem that the third commandment addresses. The welfare of society may be affected by the use of such vulgarity but does not stand or fall by combining crude expletives with the name of God.

Does this third commandment direct us then to find substitutes for the name of God so that we will choose the familiar "G-d" or "Ha-shem"(the Name), rather than writing or pronouncing the authentic name of God? What these purists fail to understand is that the name "God" in itself is a substitute for the four letter name of God found in the Torah, the ineffable title pronounced exclusively by the High Priest when he entered the Holy of Holies on the Day of Atonement. Any other name is artificially constructed and need not be altered in writing or speech.

Dennis Prager commented on this problem in *Moment* magazine (June 1998). He claims, "If God is spelled G-d, shouldn't *Hashem* be spelled "H-sh-m?" To forbid the spelling of God but allow the spelling of *Hashem* implies that "God" is a more sacred name than "*Hashem*." Prager continues: "There is a great desire among some contemporary Jews to distinguish themselves as more authentically Jewish than other Jews; calling God '*Hashem*' and writing G-d are two manifestations of this desire."

It is apparent then that the third commandment is concerned with the problem of swearing falsely under oath—committing perjury in a court of law. The only way that justice can be achieved is when those involved in litigation are willing to swear before God that their testimony is reliable; they are prepared to accept the consequences of lying under oath. To this day, truth-telling under oath remains one of the most effective ways to obtain the truth in a court of law.

Many people who reject the basic tenets of their faith do not accept the need to fear God. For them the whole concept seems alien, especially when they have been taught to associate fear with authoritarianism and coercive power. In the Book of Deuteronomy we find that the fear of God and the love of God are found together, to teach us that both attitudes are required if we are to grasp our relationship with God in our lives. The two concepts are not mutually exclusive but complementary. There are times when we are expected to love God with our whole being—our heart, our soul and our might. Yet, there are times when our love for God is not powerful enough to prevent us from violating an ethical norm, such as swearing falsely. We may believe that we are free to break rules impressed on us by the Decalogue, and as long as we profess our love for God, He will return His love unconditionally. But a mature religious belief also requires a feeling of reverence for God, implying a refusal to tamper arbitrarily with the God-given rules of moral conduct.

The language of religion, especially the translation from the original, can be misleading and confusing to those who are not at home in the Hebrew language. For example, the concept, fear of God, is frequently taken to mean that we must approach God with the same sense of trepidation with which we confront a dictatorial leader who leaves us no choice but to obey his commands. No wonder that such a misunderstanding about our relationship to God contributes to a widespread loss of faith. But the fear of God does not mean that we should approach Him with a sense of dread and helplessness. Fear of God calls for a sense of awe and reverence along with a reluctance to pursue the path of evil, but we are in no way reduced to helpless puppets in the presence of God. It would be helpful to understand our relationship with God as a form of covenant. Parties enter a covenantal relationship because they need each other, and desire to please each other in order to maintain a lasting relationship. This is the basis of God's covenant with Israel.

In an ideal society it would not be necessary to place one's hand on a Bible and swear that one's testimony is true. A "yes" or "no" would be sufficient without the requirement to take an oath and suffer the consequences of lying. But in the real world where the fear of lying under oath is still present in most people, we must rely on the time-honored practice of keeping litigants on the straight and narrow path by instilling the feeling that they are accountable to God in their testimony. They need to treat the truth as something that God requires to assure that justice is done. Those who deny a belief in God are not required to swear on the Bible, or swear at all. They are required, however, to formally affirm their intention to tell the truth. This affirmation assures the court that they understand the seriousness of what they are about to say and the binding nature of their testimony.

The Talmud goes beyond the original meaning of the third commandment in Exodus. In Berakhot (33a) the view is expressed that the recitation of a superfluous or inappropriate blessing—a *b'rakha* recited in vain—is deemed a violation of this commandment and is treated as a serious infraction of Jewish law, because God's name is included in the blessing.

The Sages were so careful to avoid a blessing recited in vain that they even introduced new customs to comply with the law. For example, the custom of eating new fruit on the second night of Rosh Hashanah was instituted to relieve any doubt that the blessing of *Sheheheyanu* ("Who has kept us in life") may be said on the second evening as well as the first. The blessing is not to be understood as a magical formula that, if recited incorrectly or without an accompanying act, would incur God's wrath. Concern for such detail was stressed to encourage an attitude of reverence for God and the utterance of His Name.

Religious thinkers continue to find new and expanded meaning to the third commandment. Here is a sampling:

Elton Trueblood, who was a distinguished Protestant teacher and preacher, presented an innovative interpretation of this commandment in his *Foundations for Reconstruction* (1946). "The third commandment does not condemn those who fail to believe; it condemns those who believe and do nothing about it. . . what is dangerous is not intellectual atheism, which is unpopular, but mild religion, which is very popular indeed." Trueblood contends that the commandment expresses the urgent need to take our beliefs more seriously.

While discussing another possible meaning of the third commandment with a friend, Doctor Sam Menahem, he suggested this valuable interpretation of the third commandment: When we ask God to fulfill a request that is either selfish or harmful, we are taking God's name in vain. God doesn't fulfill our request merely because He wishes us to feel good or to satisfy a transient wish.

Several years ago the well-known author and scholar Stephen Carter wrote *Taking God's Name in Vain*. He suggested that today's politicians who use religion and invoke God's name to receive public acclaim are guilty of taking His Name in vain.

# Insights From The Sages

## Making Vows Can Become Addictive

God said to Israel, "Be careful what you vow, and do not become addicted to making vows, for whoever is so addicted will eventually sin by breaking his oath; he who breaks his oath denies Me without hope of pardon" (Ex.20: 7).

(Tanhuma B., Mattot 79a)

## Only the Reverent Should Swear to God

Deuteronomy states, "You must revere the Lord your God: only Him shall you worship, to Him shall you hold fast, and by His name shall you swear" (10:20). You may swear only if you are a God-revering person, even as Abraham, who was so called (Gen. 22:12) or Joseph (Gen. 42:18) or Job (1:2).

(Tanhuma B., Vayikra 15)

## The Destructiveness of a False Oath

[The curse] shall enter the house of a person who swears falsely by My name...and it shall consume them to the last timber and stone"(Zechariah 5:4). Hence you learn that a false oath consumes even things that neither fire nor water can consume.

(B. Shevuot 39a)

## Beware Even of a Sincere Oath

Rabbi Judah reported in the name of Rav that, in a year of scarcity, a man deposited a gold denar with a widow, who placed it in a jar of flour. Subsequently [having forgotten about it], she baked the flour and gave[the loaf of bread] to a poor person.

In the course of time, the owner of the denar came and said to her, "Return my denar." She replied, "May death take one of my sons if I have derived any benefit for myself from your denar." Not many days passed—so it is told—before one of her sons died. When the Sages heard of the incident, they remarked: If such happens to one who swears honestly, what must be the fate of one who swears dishonestly!

(B. Gittin 35a)

זָכוֹר אֶת יוֹם הַשַּׁבָּת לְקַדְּשׁוֹ.
שֵׁשֶׁת יָמִים תַּעֲבֹד וְעָשִׂיתָ כָּל מְלַאכְתֶּךָ.
וְיוֹם הַשְּׁבִיעִי שַׁבָּת לַיהֹוָה אֱלֹהֶיךָ לֹא
תַעֲשֶׂה כָל מְלָאכָה אַתָּה וּבִנְךָ וּבִתֶּךָ
עַבְדְּךָ וַאֲמָתְךָ וּבְהֶמְתֶּךָ וְגֵרְךָ אֲשֶׁר בִּשְׁעָרֶיךָ.
כִּי שֵׁשֶׁת יָמִים עָשָׂה יְהֹוָה אֶת הַשָּׁמַיִם וְאֶת
הָאָרֶץ אֶת הַיָּם וְאֶת כָּל אֲשֶׁר בָּם
וַיָּנַח בַּיּוֹם הַשְּׁבִיעִי עַל כֵּן בֵּרַךְ יְהֹוָה אֶת
יוֹם הַשַּׁבָּת וַיְקַדְּשֵׁהוּ.

Remember the Sabbath day
and keep it holy. Six days you
shall labor and do all your work,
but the seventh day is a Sabbath
of the Lord your God; you shall
not do any work—you , your son
or daughter, your male or female
slave, or your cattle, or the stranger
who is within your settlements.
For in six days the Lord made heaven
and earth and sea, and all that is
in them, and He rested on the
Seventh day; therefore the Lord
blessed the Sabbath day and
hallowed it.

# Fourth Commandment

# Reflections

Each time I relate the story, I cannot help but chuckle, with a haevy heart. A Jew is driving around for over an hour in Jerusalem in search of a parking space. In desperation, he looks upward and vows, "If you provide me with a space for my car, dear God, I vow that I will begin to keep the holy Sabbath every week." Just as he completes his vow, he eyes someone pulling out of a precious parking space. Again he looks up and exclaims: "Never mind, dear God, I have just found myself a space." A humorous story, to be sure, and yet it reveals the difficulty that most Jews have in committing themselves to the rigorous demands of keeping the Sabbath, especially if they have never lived an observant Jewish life.

The charge to set aside the Sabbath as a day of rest and abstention from many weekday activities is the only commandment in the Decalogue that deals with religious observance. Although little mention of the intricate Sabbath ritual is found in the fourth commandment, the minute requirements of what constitutes work and rest on the Sabbath are later formulated in the Talmud and the codes of Jewish Law. The details were eventually included in the essence of the fourth commandment.

Recognition of the Sabbath as a special day among contemporary Jews varies widely, ranging from those whose lives revolve around each weekly Sabbath and who meticulously prepare for the Holy Day, as much as several days before its arrival, to those who are hardly aware that Shabbat is different from Saturday or any other day in the week. It is merely another workday or part of the weekend.

Some American Jews recognize the Sabbath by attending worship services, yet do not find the need to observe the day at home; others follow several home rituals—candle lighting, the recitation of *kiddush* over wine, a family dinner—but attend no synagogue service to commemorate the Sabbath.

In spite of its wide diversity in belief and observance, Jews tend to agree on at least three matters regarding the Sabbath: First, the origin of the Jewish Sabbath is found in the Decalogue; the Christian and Moslem Sabbaths, observed respectively on Sunday and Friday, were derived from the Jewish Sabbath and were conceived originally as a reaction to the stubborn refusal among the Jews to give up their own Sabbath on the seventh day of the week. Second, if the Sabbath is still a living institution after centuries of threats to its survival, chances are that it will continue to co-exist with the survival of the Jewish people. The final point of agreement among most Jews deserves the greatest emphasis: So long as the Sabbath is distinguished from the other six days of the week, the Jewish people will continue to survive; so long as the people survive, the Sabbath will continue to play a role in their lives. The celebrated essayist Ahad Ha-am, insightfully described this interdependence between the Jewish people and their Sabbath with these oft-quoted words: "More than the people of Israel has maintained the Sabbath, the Sabbath has maintained the people of Israel."

One of the glaring differences between the two versions of the Decalogue in Exodus and Deuteronomy is found in the fourth commandment. In Exodus the text reads: "Remember the Sabbath day and keep it holy." In Deuteronomy the expression "observe" is used rather than "remember." The difference in language appears to be deliberate; the two words convey different concepts. "Remember" implies the need to recall or set aside the Sabbath as a sacred day. "Observe" requires some form of action; more specifically, it is an exhortation to fulfill the positive requirements and to refrain from any activity forbidden on the Sabbath.

The talmudic Sages were perplexed by the apparent discrepancy of these two versions. How can a single decree from God be handed down in two different versions? The Sages concluded that "Remember and observe in the same commandment express what the human tongue cannot say and the ear cannot hear." (Rosh Hashanah 27a). Only God can express two thoughts simultaneously since He is not confined to the limitations of human speech. The Sabbath prayer *lekha dodi* also recognizes the apparent paradox with these words: "Observe" and "remember" were uttered together by our incomparable Creator.

The two versions of the fourth commandment differ in yet another way. In Exodus, the Sabbath commemorates the Creation of the world. It is a day of universal and cosmic significance. But in Deuteronomy the Sabbath is associated with the remembrance of the Exodus from Egypt; it has significance for the children of Israel, the Jewish people. In Jewish thought the universal and the particular are complementary, not exclusive of each other.

The Sabbath is one of ancient Judaism's greatest innovations. We do not know of any society prior to the Israelites that observed a day in which human beings were required to refrain from physical labor and creative activity. Most ancient societies regarded individuals as worthy only as long as they were able to work productively. That is why, for example, some Roman thinkers ridiculed the Jewish Sabbath, citing it as proof of Jewish indolence. Seneca, the first century Roman Stoic, wrote, "To spend every seventh day without doing anything means to lose a seventh part of life. Plutarch regarded the Sabbath as one of the Jews' "sordid habits." Tacitus saw the Sabbath as just another of the "sinister and shameful customs" among the Jews. It is apparent that in the ancient world the contention that humans have value even when not laboring or producing became the source of bitter resentment against the Jews in the Roman empire. It is possible that the Romans feared this revolutionary biblical idea, which was dangerously attractive to the masses and could radically challenge the privileged status of the patrician classes.

The fourth commandment also applied to slaves and even to animals. "Six days you shall labor and do all your work. But the seventh day is a Sabbath of the Lord your God; you shall not do any work; you, your son or daughter, your male or female slave, or your cattle, or the stranger who is within your settlements." (Ex.20:9-10). It is noteworthy that even in America, laborers were treated little better than animals until they were protected by labor laws.

Throughout most of the history of humankind, slaves were required to work seven days a week. They were regarded as chattel, not as humans with an independent will and mind. The Bible presents a different view of slavery. The slave, though not a free person, had to be given the opportunity to renew himself no less than the master. The reason for extending humane treatment to one's slave is clearly stated in Deuteronomy: "Remember that you were a slave in the land of Egypt and the Lord your God freed you from there with a mighty hand and outstretched arm. Therefore, the Lord your God commanded you to observe the Sabbath day."

It is entirely reasonable to ask why the Torah permitted servitude altogether. An Israelite could become a slave only when he defaulted on his debt or if he was unable to pay the penalty for stealing. He could also sell himself into slavery because of poverty. He was obligated to serve his master for only six years; in the seventh year he was offered his freedom. By limiting the years of enslavement, the Bible indicated that it did not encourage the institution of slavery and that a master could not own a slave; in fact, it recognized that the master-slave relationship was only temporary. Moreover, the master was responsible for securing the slave's future so that he should not return to slavery after being set free. "You shall not let him go empty; you shall furnish him liberally out of your flock, and out of your threshing floor, and out of your winepress. . . " (Deut.15:13-14).

As a member of his master's household, a Hebrew slave

was not only entitled to his Sabbath rest, he also partook of the Passover sacrificial meal. He was permitted to own and acquire property. His master could not abuse him physically or impose a burden that the slave could not endure. A runaway slave was required to be given refuge and not returned to his master. A slave who was physically impaired by his master was automatically released. The killing of a slave was as serious a crime as the killing of a free man, whether the perpetrator was his master or someone else. There were so many restrictions placed upon the master that the Sages cautioned the master: "He who acquires a slave acquires a master."

The heathen slave did not enjoy the same privileges as the Hebrew slave. The former became his master's property, and yet, Jewish law was also sensitive to his needs. He too was set free if he suffered physical injury by the hand of his owner. Likewise, the master who killed a heathen slave was subject to the death penalty. The non-Jewish slave also was entitled to rest on the Sabbath with the other members of his master's household.

It is fascinating to observe how the pre-eminent medieval authority Moses Maimonides dealt with the institution of slavery as found in the Bible and the Talmud. Maimonides was not free to abrogate the biblical law, but he sought to mitigate the sacred law by placing even greater responsibilities upon the master:

> "It is permitted to work a heathen slave with rigor. Though such is the rule, it is the quality of piety and the way of wisdom that a man be merciful and pursue justice and not make the yoke burdensome upon the slave or distress him; he must provide him with all his food and drink. . . The master should not disgrace them by hand or by word, because Scriptural law has delivered them only for service, not for humiliation. Nor should he shout at them or be angry with them, but listen to their complaints" (Yad, Avadim, 9:8).

In his *Guide for the Perplexed* (3:39), Maimonides reminds the master of the slave: "He ought to rise and go forth with you, be with you in the place you choose for yourself, and when fortune is good to you, do not grudge him his portion."

The Torah impresses upon us the principle that to work for six days during the week entitles us to rest on the Sabbath. This, too, is a novel concept with its source in the Decalogue: the nobility of work. Contrast this startling idea with Aristotle's praise of leisure over work for the upper class, primarily the philosophers.

For Aristotle, slaves were necessary to relieve the upper classes, the philosopher-aristocrats, from having to perform menial work. The philosophers had more important tasks to perform, namely to discuss what is good, true and beautiful. This sophisticated view advanced by Aristotle and his disciples was alien to rabbinic Judaism. The Talmud is not at all reluctant to mention the occupations of some of the most prominent rabbinical authorities, regardless of how menial these jobs were: Hillel was a wood-cutter; Rabbi Joshua, a blacksmith; Rabbi Hanina, a shoemaker; Rabbi Huna, a water-carrier. *The Ethics of the Sages* (Pirkei Avot) reminds us that, in combination with Torah study, one must also occupy himself with a worldly occupation, called *derekh eretz* (II, 2). That is the original meaning of the Hebrew phrase, although it was later expanded to mean acceptable human behavior. Why must Torah study be accompanied by a worldly occupation? To obviate sin. We remain humble and appreciative of the needs of others who must work for a living. Otherwise, the study of Torah remains an abstraction, a form of mental gymnastics. *Melakhah Melukhah* is a well-known Hebrew expression conveying an essential Jewish value that nobility is found in labor; even menial work should not be frowned upon. To reiterate, this emphasis on work during the week entitles one to enjoy the gift of Sabbath rest at the end of the work-week. We are reminded of the modern aphorism, "No pain, no gain."

We cannot be certain how the Sabbath was observed before the giving of the Ten Commandments. We do know that in ancient Babylonia certain days of the month were regarded as "evil days," or days associated with bad luck. Officials were not supposed to perform their usual duties on those days they called *shapattu*. It has been suggested that perhaps the biblical Sabbath was modeled after the Babylonian *shapattu*. It is possible that both institutions were derived from a more ancient common source and then developed in their own ways, according to the biblical scholar William Hallo.

In this spirit, we are also indebted to Thomas Cahill who wrote *The Gifts of the Jews* (Nan A. Talese Doubleday), one of the best-selling books to appear in 1998. Cahill wrote with passion about the Jewish Sabbath. He observed that no ancient society before the Jewish people enjoyed a day of rest. The God who created the world and then "rested" bids us to follow His example, calling us to a weekly restoration of prayer, study and recreation (or re-creation). "In this study (or *talmud*), we have the beginnings of what Nahum Sarna has called 'the universal day of continuous self-education,' Israel being the first society to so value education and the first to envision it as a universal pursuit—and a democratic obligation that those in power must safeguard on behalf of those in their employ" (p.144).

Cahill concluded his segment on the Jewish Sabbath with these poignant words: "The Sabbath is surely one of the simplest and sanest recommendations any god has ever made; and those who live without such septimal punctuations are emptier and less resourceful."

There is a Hebrew expression that one should accept a truth from whoever declares it. It is axiomatic that a true or wise thought may be conveyed by a Jew or Gentile, or even by a religious skeptic. Jethro, the Midianite priest, imparted his wisdom to his son-in-law Moses. Jethro saved Moses from burnout when he advised him to appoint assistant judges. Other scholars believe that Jethro's influence extended far beyond administrative advice in the form of wisdom and moral insight as well to his grateful son-in-law.

Abraham Heschel, in his charming yet powerful little volume *The Sabbath* emphasizes another innovative, if not revolutionary thought regarding the Jewish day of rest. All ancient civilizations with the exception of Israel identified holiness and sanctity with a particular place—a mound, a hill, a mountain, a tree, a grove, a river. There they would offer their sacrifices and/or prayers to their deities. The Jews were restricted from worshiping objects or places that occupied space. They were taught that only time, and not space, was imbued with holiness. The seasons of the year were regarded as holy. And most significantly, the holy Sabbath was a "shrine in time."

That is why the Sabbath is even more indispensable than a synagogue building—an object that occupies space. To be sure, the synagogue is essential to Jewish survival, yet individual synagogues are man-made structures with limited durability. Neighborhoods change; one synagogue may be forced to merge with another. But the Sabbath, which exists in time, is not subject to obsolescence. The Sabbath resides in the orbit of eternity.

Here are Heschel's own words: "This, then, is the answer to the problem of civilization: not to flee from the realm of space; to work with things of space, but to be in love with eternity. Things are our tools; eternity, the Sabbath is our mate."

Heschel's brilliant observation on time vs. space in the Jewish tradition may be found in the Torah itself. When the Israelites begin to build a tabernacle in the wilderness, they are reminded that even as they construct a House dedicated to God, they must give priority to the holy Sabbath: "*Six days shall work be done, but on the seventh day there shall be to you a holy day, a Sabbath of complete rest to the Lord.*"

Among many other ancient peoples, their holy days were filled either with fear and trepidation, lest they displease their deities, or they were replete with orgies and bouts of drunkenness—most often celebrated in the precincts of the temple. In stark contrast to both extremes of fear and frivolity on pagan festivals, the Jewish Sabbath required a middle course. The biblical verse, "You shall not kindle a fire in all your habitation on the Sabbath" (Ex. 35:3), was not understood as an order to sit in darkness during the Sabbath; the Sages permitted the kindling of lights *before* the Sabbath for the benefit of enjoying comfort and delight on the Sabbath. *Light* was and is synonymous with *delight*. Therefore, to sit in darkness would deny the celebrants the joy of *oneg Shabbat*, Sabbath delight.

Likewise the verse, "Let everyone remain where he is; let no man leave his place on the Sabbath," was never understood literally by Pharisaic Judaism. This verse, found in Exodus 16:29, is taken to mean that the people need not remain within their homes, but that they should not walk outside the city limits. The Sabbath was meant to be a day of family celebration, not a day given over to traveling long distances, even by foot.

Jewish law prohibited mourning on the Sabbath, unlike some of the pagan observances on their holy days. Fasting is not permitted with the exception of Yom Kippur—the "Sabbath of Sabbaths"—when it falls on a Sabbath. Wearing one's finest clothes, drinking wine, serving frugal meals if necessary during the week in order to eat one's most sumptuous meals on the Sabbath, enjoying sexual intimacy with one's partner— these are all more than mere suggestions. They are prescribed by the framers of the *halakhah*, Jewish law. Their intention apparently was to steer a middle course by avoiding the pitfalls of morbidity on the one hand and unrestricted pleasure on the other.

Yet another innovative idea is associated with the Sabbath. I have frequently asked adult students why they think that Jewish law did not permit one to ride in a wagon on the Sabbath. Invariably most students respond that the process of hitching the horse(s) to the wagon requires physical labor which is forbidden on the day of rest. Very few students are aware of the primary reason for the prohibition: *shema yahtokh zemorah*, meaning, one may break a branch or twig on the ground while riding, or reach up and break it off a tree.

The renowned psychoanalyst Erich Fromm wrote with passion about the profound meaning of the Jewish Sabbath. In his book, *You Shall Be As Gods* (Fawcett Publishers), Fromm analyzes the significance of work as it relates to the Sabbath. "Work" is any interference by man, be it constructive or destructive, with the physical world. "Rest" is a state of peace between man and nature. Man must leave nature untouched, not change it in any way, either by building or destroying anything. . . "Work" is any kind of disturbance of the man-nature equilibrium. On the basis of this general definition, we can understand the Sabbath ritual (p. 154).

On the Sabbath we are encouraged to become especially conscious of the environment, God's magnificent handiwork. We are bidden to conserve, to preserve our natural resources. That is why such a simple act as plucking a flower rather than gazing at it and appreciating its natural beauty is not acceptable on the Sabbath day. We are required to reinforce and restore that delicate balance between humanity and nature. Anything that tends to disturb that essential balance, especially on the Sabbath, is not seen as *shabbosdig*, in the spirit of the Sabbath.

The development of the Jewish Sabbath is just one example of the creativity of Judaism with its remarkable ability to be aware of alien ideas and practices in other cultures and transform them into uniquely Jewish traditions. Thus, the Jewish Sabbath was radically transformed into a day of prayer, learning and rest, a joyous family day, everything but a day associated with morbidity and bad luck which it may have originally been.

Likewise the Festival of Lights—Hanukkah—was very possibly infuenced by pagan antecedents who would light bonfires during the long winter night in an attempt to hold back the darkness. The Jews created their own Festival of Lights without the fear and magic that was previously associated with it. The lights came to be identified with an historical event—a victory performed by a small band of Maccabees over a powerful enemy, the Syrian-Greek army, that was intent on eliminating the unique religious practices of the Jewish people.

Perhaps we can better understand why the mystics saw in the Sabbath day a foretaste of the Messianic Age. The prophet Isaiah declares, in anticipation of the Messianic Age, that the breach between man and nature, between the human and animal world will be healed. The predatory wolf and the gentle lamb will enjoy co-existence. The leopard will lie down next to the kid. The calf and the beast of prey shall feed with a little boy to herd them. The lion, like the ox, shall eat straw. A young child shall play over a viper's hole, and an infant shall pass his hand over an adder's den (Chapter 11).

So the harmonious and healing spirit of the Sabbath is meant to serve as preparation for the Great Sabbath, the Age of the Messiah, when fierce competition will yield to harmony among individuals and nations. Hostility and hatred will become obsolete. This bold concept of the Sabbath viewed as a preparation for the ideal age prompted a Sage to claim that if all Israel were to fully observe two consecutive Sabbaths, then they would be redeemed (Shabbat 118b).

When the Jews, especially those living in Eastern Europe before the Holocaust, suffered constant humiliation by their adversaries, no other "vaccine" immunized them more effectively than their weekly Sabbath. During the week they were forced to bear their inferiority status on the street and in the market place. But when they gathered together with their families every Sabbath eve and welcomed the "Sabbath bride" in song and prayer, their Jewish pride and self-confidence was again restored. They were convinced that to live as a Jew even in a hostile environment meant to wear a badge of honor and pride.

Few people were able to depict this total transformation of the Sabbath Jew more passionately than the gifted poet Heinrich Heine. In his "Princess Sabbath," Heine writes of a dog turning into a prince on the Sabbath.

> Here I sing of such a prince.
> He is known as Israel.
> Words of witchcraft have transformed him,
> Turning him into a dog.
>
> As a dog, with dog-ideas
> All week long he goes on scraping
> Through life's excrement and sweepings,
> To the mocking jeers of street-boys.
>
> But on every Friday evening,
> At the hour of dusk, the magic
> Suddenly grows weak; the dog
> Once again becomes a person.

Human, and with human feeling,
With uplifted head and heart,
Clean and festively attired,
Enters he his father's dwelling.

"Greetings, O beloved dwelling
Of my mighty royal father!
Jacob's tents, upon your sacred
Entrance-posts I press my lips."

(*The Poetry and Prose of Heinrich Heine*. New York:
Citadel Press, 1948, p. 264)

# Insights from the Sages

## The Sabbath Is given a Partner

It was taught by Rabbi Shim'on bar Yohai: The Sabbath protested before the Holy One: "Sovereign of the universe! Everything has a partner, but I have no partner!" The Holy One responded: "The congregation of Israel will be your partner." Thus, when Israel stood before Mount Sinai, the Holy One reminded them: "Remember what I told Shabbat: The congregation of Israel will be your partner." This is the meaning of the commandment, "Remember the Sabbath day to sanctify it (i.e., be wedded to it)."

(Beresheet Rabbah 11:9)

## The Sabbath Satisfies Both Mind and Heart

Rabbi Berekhiah said in the name of Rabbi Hiya bar Abba: The Sabbath was given only for rejoicing. Rabbi Haggai said in the name of Shmuel bar Nahman: The Sabbath was given only for the study of Torah. There is no contradiction between them, for what Rabbi Berekhiah said about rejoicing refers to scholars, who labor in Torah all the days of the week—and on the Sabbath, they rejoice. What Rabbi Haggai said about study of Torah refers to workers, who labor at their trade all week long, but on the Sabbath they come and study Torah.

(Pesikta Rabbati [Yale J. S.] p. 490)

## God's Business Permitted on The Sabbath

Rabbi Hisda and Rabbi Hamnuna said that it is permitted to make plans for good deeds on the Sabbath, and Rabbi Elazar said that one may arrange for alms to the poor on the Sabbath. Rabbi Johanan said: One may transact business involving the saving of life or dealing with public health on the Sabbath; one may also go to the synagogue to discuss the public affairs on the Sabbath. Rabbi Jonathan said: One may even go to theaters and circuses on the Sabbath for such a purpose. And in the school of Manasseh it was said that one may talk about the future of one's children on the Sabbath, or about the children's education, or about teaching them a handicraft, for Scripture forbids "your business," but God's business is permitted.

( Shabbat 150a)

## Saving a Life Supersedes the Sabbath

One who is attacked by robbers may break the Sabbath in order to save his life. Once it happened that letters from the Roman government, containing evil tidings for the Jews, reached the elders of Sepphoris. They came and asked Rabbi Eleazar ben Perata what to do. It was on the Sabbath, and they asked, "Shall we flee?" He was afraid to tell them directly to flee on the Sabbath, so he said, "Do you ask me? Ask Jacob or Moses or David." [They were forced to flee from their adversaries.] Danger to life annuls the Sabbath, for a person is to live by fulfilling God's commandments, and not die by them. The law of circumcision annuls the Sabbath. Now if something affecting a single one of man's organs annuls the Sabbath, how much more must the Sabbath be annulled when his life, which involves all his 248 parts, is affected.

(Tanhuma B. Mas'ey 81a)

## The Sabbath Produces Its Own Aroma

The Emperor asked Rabbi Joshua ben Hananiah, "What gives your Sabbath meat such an aroma?" He replied, "We have a spice called Shabbat, which is put in the cooking of the meat; this gives it its aroma." The Emperor said, "Give me some of this spice." He replied, "For those who keep the Sabbath the spice works; for those who do not keep it, it does not work."

(B. Shabbat 119a)

כַּבֵּד אֶת אָבִיךָ וְאֶת אִמֶּךָ
לְמַעַן יַאֲרִכוּן יָמֶיךָ עַל
הָאֲדָמָה אֲשֶׁר יְהֹוָה
אֱלֹהֶיךָ נֹתֵן לָךְ .

Honor your father and your mother,
that you may long endure on the land
that the Lord your God is assigning
to you.

# Fifth Commandment

# Reflections

It is generally understood that the first half of the Decalogue deals with one's relationship to God (*beyn adam la-Makom*), and the second half is directed to one's relationship with his fellow human beings (*beyn adam le-havero*). But why is the commandment to honor one's parents placed with the first and not the second set of commandments? Merely to rationalize that we would sacrifice the need for symmetry were the fifth commandment shifted to the second set fails to take into account the unique moral message conveyed by the fifth commandment: It serves as the linking commandment between the two sections of the Decalogue. In honoring one's parents, the son or daughter also pays homage to God; the failure to show respect for one's parents is tantamount to a denial of reverence for God.

A renowned Tanna of the Mishnah, Rabbi Shimon bar Yohai, observed that the fifth commandment was the most difficult among other difficult commandments to fulfill (Tanhuma B.3). In theory, we should regard filial respect as normal and natural—after all, parents have given us life, nourished us and taught us how to love. But, the complexity of human behavior does not usually operate in such a predictable and rational way.

I remember how impressed I was when I first learned the

talmudic principle that one must not impose a rule of conduct that is too difficult for the majority to follow. Now, if the command to honor parents is so difficult to fulfill, why was it proclaimed in the first place? The fifth commandment appears to be an exception to the talmudic principle. In spite of the extreme effort required to observe the fifth commandment, it should nevertheless be viewed as an ideal, a standard that the child can aspire to. Otherwise, the household could be reduced to a state of anarchy resulting in the breakdown of relationships within the family structure and the failure to pass down valued family traditions.

But why should honoring one's parents be so difficult, so unnatural? For the most part, parents and children have conflicting needs. Many parents want their children to remain close even in adulthood; they prefer to see them in the same compliant role as they were during their dependent years.

Growing children, however, develop a different agenda for themselves. They feel that they must forge their own identity even if it requires independence from their elders who are still dear to them. They feel that they must find their own way even if their parents may be able to help them avoid major mistakes, say, in the choice of an incompatible partner or an impractical business venture. The parents find it difficult to appreciate the child's need to separate, even to move to a remote area, especially when the parents insist on offering their unsolicited advice, which is often understood as unwelcome interference.

One would think that this generational conflict is a contemporary problem which did not exist in close traditional families where there was little opportunity for experimentation or rebellion. But Rabbi Shimon bar Yohai indicated that these parent-child conflicts were prevalent in the talmudic era. And long before his time, the first Hebrew, Abraham, could never have become the founder of a new nation had he not been able to exert his individuality to the displeasure of his father Terah. Legend has it that Terah was a maker of idols. How could his son, the discoverer of ethical monotheism, not clash with his father on this crucial principle of religious belief? Abraham could no longer remain the compliant son under the close supervision of his father, and simultaneously strike out on his own with his life's partner, Sarah. Both parent and child frequently experience the pangs of separation, but without separation, maturity and growth are most difficult to achieve.

The fifth commandment is clearly stated in a positive fashion for the benefit of each subsequent generation of sons and daughters struggling for self-reliance, for their own voice, yet appreciative of their parents' sincere intentions and their experience and wisdom. Elsewhere in the Torah we find several connected laws such as the prohibitions against dishonoring one's elders, cursing or hitting a parent, acting out one's hostility as a stubborn and rebellious son, etc.

The Talmud (B. Kiddushin 30b) questions why the Decalogue mentions the father before the mother. The response given is that a son may tend to honor his mother more than his father, since she may win him over with kind words. To correct this possible tendency, the father is mentioned first. In Leviticus, however, we are required to "revere every man his *mother* and *father* " (Lev. 19:3). Here the mother is mentioned first because the son may tend to revere his father more, since he was traditionally the disciplinarian in the family. Therefore, the mother is here mentioned first to emphasize the reverence that is also her due. Both parents are given equal emphasis. Parenthetically, the verse in Leviticus requiring reverence for mother and father is followed by the command, "and keep my Sabbaths." As in the Decalogue, so here in Leviticus, the two commandments are in close proximity, although the order is reversed in Leviticus. The Torah appears to be teaching us that there is a relationship between honoring the Sabbath and honoring parents: Observing the Sabbath together as a weekly family celebration can help instill greater respect and honor toward one's parents. Finding one's parents in a relaxed and informal mood around the Sabbath table tends to promote mutual warmth and openness to genuine dialogue.

I have frequently been asked why the fifth commandment deals specifically with a child's obligation toward the parents. Why was it not a more general command, such as the need to honor elders, which would include parents? Why was the command not expanded to include the senior citizens in the community, many of whom fail to receive respect and attention from the younger generation? The command to honor the elderly—"You must rise before the aged"—is mentioned elsewhere in Leviticus. The purpose of the Decalogue is not intended to be an all-inclusive document, but to deal with the minimal requirements essential to a moral society. The Torah recognizes that the child comes most frequently in contact with parents, especially in the earlier years. He/she usually learns to show deference to teachers and to the aged as a result of developing a wholesome relationship with one's parents. The home environment serves as a vital passageway to the neighborhood and the larger community.

But let us suppose that a parent has not earned respect and honor from the child. He/she may have physically and emotionally abused the child over the years. Or the child has sadly observed how one of the parents has exploited the other parent. Can the mere presence of a commandment prevent the child from feeling justified resentment? Does the child have any moral obligation to honor a selfish or self-centered parent?

This is where some of the other charges in the Torah can instruct the child. You may not be able to honor your parent with your affection; still you are not free to abuse the parent physically or verbally. The child has minimal obligations even toward an unworthy parent.

The Sages go to great lengths to emphasize respect for parents even when the parents err. For example, a child sees his father transgress a law of the Torah. The child must not say to him, "You have violated the words of the Torah." Rather should he say: "Father, is it not written in the Torah thus and thus?" This he should do as if he were inquiring rather than blaming him, and his parent would understand and not be put to shame.

Though respect for parents is equated with honoring God, Jewish tradition understands that a child's obedience to parents should not be blind or unconditional. These are some of the exceptions found in rabbinic sources: If the parent insists that the child violate the Sabbath, the child should not obey. He is expected to follow the divine law explicitly written in the Decalogue. Likewise, if a child desires to leave home in order to study Torah because the instruction in another place is superior, he may leave, even if the parents are unhappy with the child's decision. The duty to study Torah takes priority over the wishes of parents. Jewish law is also explicit about the child's wish to settle in the land of Israel although the parents may object to the child's resolve. The mitzvah of making *aliyah*, a permanent home in Israel, is given even higher priority than honoring the wishes of parents.

In spite of these glaring exceptions set down by Jewish authorities, it is clearly understood before the child is free to make an independent decision that he/she should be mature enough to act responsively; that the child is not merely looking for an escape from the family; that the child is not exposing himself/herself to a dangerous environment; that the child can support himself/herself financially should the parents refuse to offer support.

It is apparent from these exceptions that respect and honor do not operate only in one direction, from child to parent. Parents should not arbitrarily set rigid rules for their children to follow merely to test their loyalty. Nor should they force them to choose between parents and teachers. The Jewish tradition regards parents primarily as teachers of their young, but when they neglect their responsibility to provide them with moral or spiritual direction, they abdicate their parental rights and privileges. They invite disagreement and resentment.

Although the commandment to honor parents is equated with honoring God, the Torah does not explicitly require the child to feel or express love for parents, only respect. You cannot legislate love, especially when parents have shown themselves to be undeserving of a child's love. Even to expect a son or daughter victimized by an abusive parent to show respect for the parent can be unreasonable and unrealistic.

I was recently confronted with this very problem when I was invited to officiate at a wedding in the south. The bride-to-be requested that I omit the name of her father from the *ketubah*, the Jewish marriage document, because he abandoned her mother and two children and placidly stepped out of their lives. She gave much serious thought to her request: "Why should I show him affection or love. He made a choice many years ago and our small family had to put our lives together without him. He did not literally die. But my love for him died." I had no recourse but to follow her wishes. She could not be told that she was required to feel love or affection for an absentee parent who had left her family impoverished and demoralized for several crucial years in her young life.

A woman whom I had known for many years came to my study with a bitter complaint against her son-in-law who consistently belittled her. He relished all the mother-in-law jokes, relating them to anyone who would provide him an audience. When she finally mustered the courage to confront him, he insisted that he meant her no harm; he advised her not to take his brand of humor as a personal affront.

The offended woman then posed a question which I had never anticipated. She deserved a direct answer, if there was one. She wanted to know if the commandment to honor one's parents included in-laws as well. I admitted to her that I had never given serious thought to her question, but that I would do some research and return to her in a few days.

I returned with the response that I seriously doubted that the fifth commandment originally intended to include in-laws. Yet, we do find in the *Mekhilta* (Sec. 3) this revealing Midrash: Moses showed honor to his father-in-law, as it is said: "And Moses went and returned to Jethro, his father-in-law" (Ex.4:18). Now, his father-in-law showed honor to him. When people asked him, "What is your distinction?" he would say to them, "I am the father-in-law of Moses." Two comments are in order. First, the text here uses the same verb, k-b-d (honor), as we find in the Decalogue, which emphasizes the need to extend the same honor to in-laws as to one's own parents. Second, the text implies that if honor is extended to one's in-laws, the same honor will probably be reciprocated to the son or daughter-in-law.

Although the moral lesson found in this midrashic passage was not included in the Code of Jewish law, respect for in-laws is nevertheless regarded as a meritorious act and should be taken seriously. Hostile jokes at the expense of in-laws may evoke laughter from an audience at the comedy club, but they do not serve the best interests of creating closeness within the family.

The fifth commandment does not specifically address the issue of paying respect to grandparents, yet, we may certainly infer that they are no less deserving of respect than one's own parents. By virtue of their more advanced age and their need for recognition and attention, the reminder to honor grandparents should not be taken for granted.

I have observed many young adults who treat their grandparents with greater deference than their own parents. They appear to relate to grandparents more freely and share their personal problems more openly with the elder generation. The grandparents are, more often than not, less demanding, less judgmental and may be approached without conditions. The relationship with grandparents carries less emotional baggage than between parent and child, which is understandable, given the complex generational problems among many contemporary families.

Although a strong bond between grandparent and grandchild should be encouraged, it should not be understood as a valid substitute for a wholesome parent-child relationship. Grandparents would be wise not to attempt to exploit their role but to promote greater harmony between child and parent, especially if they can exert a positive influence on the grandchild.

By the same token, parents of young children should not deny grandparents the right and privilege of visiting their grandchildren even when a strained relationship exists between the first and second generation. Much has been written on the subject in recent years; several cases have come before the courts regarding the issue of visitation rights that were denied to grandparents because of family feuding. Generally the courts have shown sympathy for the emotional needs of grandparents.

Denial of visitations to grandparents can be used as a vengeful weapon with serious consequences for the aggrieved grand-parents and their grandchildren. Such drastic action should be taken only under these extreme circumstances: when grand-parents attempt to destroy a normal relationship between par-ent and child or to instill harmful moral values in the mind of the grandchild. A distinction should be made between instilling *different* values and *destructive* values that could result in a rupture of relations between parents and their children. Under such turbulent conditions, parents have the right to make the critical decision on behalf of their child, although it should be arrived at after much soul-searching along with professional consultation.

Yet another vital question needs to be explored under the rubric of the fifth commandment: Is it permissible in Jewish law to institutionalize a parent with a debilitating illness? Pro-fessor David Golinkin, president of the Schechter Institute of Jewish Studies in Jerusalem, wrote a responsum on this prob-lem for *Moment* magazine. Golinkin first cites the authority of the Ra'avad who interprets the fifth commandment as an ab-solute. The child is personally obligated to care for his parents and must not leave them all the days of his life, regardless of the parent's condition.

Others, following the view of the master legal authority, Moses Maimonides, claim that the child is not *personally* ob-ligated to physically care for the parent, if he must sacrifice his own emotional well being. Furthermore, in cases of advanced mental deterioration, such as Alzheimer's disease, an outsider may prove to be more effective than the adult child.

Golinkin suggests that the views of both great authorities could be accommodated: the parent may be kept at home in familiar and comfortable surroundings; the child may pay an outsider to attend to functions which are too painful for him to perform. By maintaining the parent at home, the child literally fulfills the commandment to "honor your father and mother," as the Ra'avad requires. And following Maimonides, the child protects the parent's honor and his own emotional health by ensuring that a professional is present to assist the child (Golinkin, David, *Responsa in a Moment*, pp. 39-41, April 1991).

The fifth commandment, unlike most of the other commandments listed in the Torah, promises a reward: length of days. Only two biblical laws, when they are fulfilled, promise to deliver the blessing of longevity: honoring parents and driving away a mother bird from her nest before taking either the fledglings or the eggs. The moral purpose of both commands is obvious, but offering an equal reward to both is difficult to comprehend. Honoring one's parents appears to deserve greater reward than sparing the pain that one may inflict upon a bird. But apparently the Bible wants to teach us an essential lesson, namely, that we humans are unable to determine for ourselves what moral laws God considers more significant than others. Avoiding emotional pain to animals is not to be taken lightly just because birds do not share the status of humans on the evolutionary ladder. The "feelings" of all God's creatures deserve our consideration.

There are various ways in which we may interpret the reward, "that you may long endure on the land which the Lord your God is giving you." I prefer to regard the meaning of the reward for honoring parents in the form of spiritual compensation: Your days will be fulfilled. You will anticipate each new day free of the feelings of guilt that so often accompanies filial neglect of parents. In addition, honoring the aged, and especially one's parents, contributes to the preservation of the entire social fabric; rejecting the needs of one's parents in their old age imperils the spiritual health of our society.

We have experienced dramatic changes in the way that some elderly parents have come to be regarded, especially in our age of affluence. There was a time when adult children would be most reluctant to move to another part of the country, leaving their aging parent(s) to fend for themselves or to be placed into a depressing nursing facility. Even setting them up in an apartment in a warm climate separated from their natural family, and especially the grandchildren, may not serve the real emotional needs of many aged parents.

Abraham Joshua Heschel presented a paper before the White House Conference on Aging in 1961, which he entitled "To Grow in Wisdom." His poignant message is no less relevant today, more than four decades after it was delivered. "The test of a people is how it behaves toward the old. It is easy to love children. Even tyrants and dictators make a point of being fond of children. But the affection and care for the old, the incurable, the helpless are the true gold mines of a culture. . . We maintain that all men are created equal, including the old. What is extraordinary is that we feel called upon to plead for such equality, in contrast to other civilizations in which the superiority of the old is maintained" (*The Insecurity of Freedom*, p. 72).

For centuries Jewish tradition has provided a mechanism to honor parents not only in life but also after they die. Children are required to attend religious services daily for eleven months and on the anniversary of the parents' death. At the religious service the survivors recite the Mourner's Kaddish in which they confront their personal loss with an affirmation of faith in God even in the face of tragedy. As people become more involved in the demands of their business and professional activities, they are less inclined to maintain this religious requirement for a long period. This is especially true for those who travel extensively—they often find reason to neglect this hallowed Jewish tradition. "I honored my father in life. Why then must I extend my responsibility beyond the grave?" Another common rationalization: "Knowing my mother, I don't think she would have wanted me to go to such lengths to prove that I remain a dutiful son after her death."

These arguments may sound convincing and not easy to refute. True, the respect that parents should receive in their lifetime takes precedence over the honor due them after death. Yet, Jewish tradition does not exempt the fulfilment of one mitzvah in place of the other. We cannot but wonder if parents, even without a strong religious commitment, would want to discourage their children from the recitation of Kaddish. In my forty-three years in the active rabbinate I never heard a parent express the view that the Kaddish was trivial or that I should advise the survivors not to recite Kaddish after his/her death.

Kaddish is not a personal prayer or meditation sent up to the deceased parent—a common misconception. It is not officially a prayer at all. It is more of an affirmation that at a time of personal grief we are willing to proclaim in the midst of a quorum, a *minyan*, the belief that God's world is governed by justice. It is one of various ways that the worshiper may publicly perform an act of *Kiddush Hashem*, sanctification of God's name. The regimen of attendance at a religious service for eleven months also gives the mourner an opportunity to re-affirm ties to the synagogue and with one's fellow worshipers who are expected to respond to the recitation of the Mourn-er's Kaddish. The mourner not only shows honor to the de-ceased parent, but also faith in the need to perpetuate one of the primary purposes of the Synagogue, creating a bond of fellowship among worshipers.

Honoring the memory of parents after their death is not confined to the daily recitation of the *Kaddish*, as demanding as that discipline may be for the mourner. What is far more difficult is the ability to forgive parents who deeply hurt us when they were alive, parents who withheld from us their warmth and sympathy when we needed it most. So many adult sons and daughters perpetuate bitter feelings toward their de-ceased parents throughout their own lives, finding justification for their bitterness. One woman summed up her unrelieved hostility to her long-deceased mother: "Why should I be a hyp-ocrite? How can I even attempt to say that I now forgive her after I was made to feel so inferior to my sisters?"

It is a given that the deep scars left with a child cannot vanish simply by a gesture of forgiveness. And yet, by perpet-uating hostility even after a parent has been laid to rest, the unforgiving child does not allow himself to find closure and the opportunity to move forward. The resentful child continues to retard his own emotional growth and maturity. Uncontrolled hostility and anger, especially based on feelings of deprivation in childhood, whether real or imagined, keeps the living heirs imprisoned, enslaved to the memories of their unfortunate child-hood. Although it is unrealistic to demand love of a hurtful parent, forgiveness of that parent becomes one of the most humane and spiritual acts that a person can perform precisely *because* it is so difficult to achieve, and yet the reward is so perceptible.

By the same token, asking forgiveness of departed parents for our own unintended or deliberate abuse is just as commendable as the act of forgiving parents who have hurt us. To seek forgiveness of parents no matter how long they have been separated from us can impress upon us the timeless message that honoring parents carries no statute of limitations. It is never too late to make amends for our youthful indiscretions.

Although the deceased parents are unable to respond to the regretful child or to pardon the child verbally, it is the son or daughter who feels liberated by acknowledging the pain that they may have caused their parents during their lifetime. Among Jewish families it has been a longstanding tradition for children to go to the cemetery before the holy days or on the anniversary of the parent's death and ask their forgiveness for hurts inflicted on them.

A recurring question: But why must we wait until after parents are laid to rest before forgiving them or seeking their forgiveness? Of course a child deserves greater merit when forgiveness is extended or asked for while the parents are yet alive. The parents have the satisfaction of reacting to the child's generosity of spirit or his/her act of genuine contrition. But the human personality is too complex to conform to a prescribed timetable. Whether the commandment is fulfilled when it is most appropriate—during the parents' lifetime—or even after the death of the parents, we can appreciate the strategic placement of the commandment in the center of the Decalogue. With economy of words and unmistakable clarity the message serves to impress upon each succeeding generation the timelessness and relevance of the fifth commandment.

# Insights From the Sages

## God Is Intimidated by the Disrespectful Child

When a person curses his father and mother, or strikes them, leaving bruises on them, the Holy One draws His feet back [in revulsion]under the throne of glory, if one dare say such a thing, as He declares: "I made his honoring parents equal to honoring Me. Had I been dwelling with this person, he could have done the same to Me. I do well not to live in the same house with such a person."

(Tanna de-Bei Eliyyahu (JPS) p.331)

## Even a Poor Child Must Help a Needy Parent

Rabbi Shimon bar Yohai said: "Great is the duty of honoring one's father and mother, since the Holy One set the honor due them above the honor due to Himself. For concerning the honor due to the Holy One, it is written, "Honor the Lord with your substance" (Proverbs 3:9). How does one honor God with his substance? One sets aside gleanings, forgotten sheaves, and the corners of the field. . . One takes a lulav, builds a sukkah, uses a shofar, tefillin and ritual fringes, one feeds the hungry, gives drink to the thirsty, and clothes the naked. In short, if you have the means, you are obligated to do all these things; but if you are without substance, you are not obliged to do even one of them. When it comes to honoring father and mother, however, whether you have substance or not, what does Scripture say? 'Honor your father and your mother,' even if you must go about begging in doorways."

(Pesikta Rabbati [Yale J.S.] p. 499)

## The Mother's Right to Be Saved First

Our masters taught: When a man, and his father, and his teacher are in captivity, he has the first right to be ransomed before his teacher, and his teacher before his father. But his mother has the first right to be ransomed before all of them.

(B. Horayot 13a)

## Postponing a Request from a Parent

Eleazar ben Matia stated: "If my father says, 'Give me a drink of water,' while I have a precept to fulfill, I must put aside the honor due my father and perform the precept, since both I and my father are obligated by the precept." But Isi ben Judah added a reservation: "If the precept can be fulfilled by others, then let them perform it, while the son attends his parent's honor."

(B. Kiddushin 32a)

## When Saying No to a Parent Is a Mitzvah

"You shall revere every man his mother and his father" (Lev. 19:3). One might suppose then that if a father [who is a priest] says to his son [also a priest], "Defile yourself [by coming in contact with the dead]," or "Do not return a lost article," the son must obey his father. Therefore, Scripture says, "You shall revere every man his mother and his father," followed immediately by "And you shall keep My Sabbaths: I am the Lord your God." This implies that all of you are bound to honor Me first.

(B. Yevamot 6a)

# Preface to the Second Set of Commandments

Although the Decalogue is usually thought of as an indivisible unit, it does not require much investigation to detect glaring substantive and linguistic differences between the commandments found on the first and second tablets. The first section deals with the more abstract topics, such as belief in God's existence and the profound meaning of the Sabbath. The second tablet deals with tangible and recognizable interpersonal transgressions, such as theft and lying and murder. The first set of commands is more verbose; the second set is known for its direct style, its economy of words. The second section consists exclusively of negative commands; the first section contains both positive and negative directives.

What is most striking is that each of the first set of commands contains God's name, whereas mention of God is absent throughout the second set. We cannot be certain whether the omission was deliberate. One thing is certain, however, and that is the absence of God's name was not meant to place less value on the second half of the Decalogue. What other commandment could be more critical than *You shall not murder?* Is it possible that the force of this command automatically conjures up a feeling of awe and trepidation that is associated with the divine imperative, perhaps eliminating the need to be re-enforced by mention of God's name? Does the use of God's name in itself assure that a command will be taken with a sense of greater urgency? One is reminded of the Book of Esther that does not contain the divine name and yet the book was incorporated into the sacred Hebrew Bible. God's presence was *felt* in the book, especially when Mordecai solemnly reminds his niece Esther, "If you keep silent in this crisis (Haman's plan to exterminate the Jews) relief and deliverance will come to the Jews from another quarter. . ."(Book of Esther 4:14). There is little doubt that Mordecai intended to instill a sense of awe in Esther's heart even without referring overtly to God. And it worked. Esther got the message.

לֹא תִּרְצָח.

You shall not murder.

# Sixth Commandment

# Reflections

When I first memorized the Decalogue as a young child, I recited the sixth commandment incorrectly, just as I was taught by my Sunday School teacher: "Thou shalt not kill." It took me years to realize that the text was directed at the sin of premeditated or deliberate murder. Although the Torah prohibited taking the law into one's own hands, it did not rule out capital punishment handed down by a court of law. Neither did it forbid taking another's life in self-defense or in warfare. Theoretically, though rarely carried out, a person could be executed for adultery or homosexual practices. So, in the biblical period, judicial executions were not only sanctioned but were thought to reflect God's will. The rabbinic law, which developed over a period of centuries following the biblical era, goes into great detail to explain how the different methods of execution were carried out by the Jewish court, how many judges were needed to decide in capital cases, etc.

We have no way of knowing how often capital punishment was invoked in the rabbinic period. But there seems to be sufficient evidence in the Talmud that the death penalty was infrequently applied after the destruction of Jerusalem in the year 70 C.E.

The law demanded two witnesses to a crime, a requirement that prevented almost all cases from coming to trial. The witnesses were questioned separately regarding the exact place and time of the crime and their recognition of the accused. If there was any discrepancy in their testimony, the accused was immediately acquitted. Furthermore, the witnesses had to warn the accused that he was about to commit a crime that carried the death penalty. The accused had to reject the warning and proceed to commit the criminal act fully conscious of the nature and consequences of his crime.

Once the case came before the judges, a majority of one was sufficient to acquit the accused; a plurality of two was required to convict. Furthermore, there had to be at least one judge in the court of twenty-three to argue in favor of acquittal. If the decision to convict was unanimous, collusion was suspected. Unlike the case with non-capital crimes, a judge who voted for acquittal could not then change his vote for conviction, yet he was free to change his vote from conviction to acquittal. A verdict to acquit could be handed down on the same day of the trial, but not a verdict of conviction, which required more deliberation.

Once the death sentence was pronounced, every consideration was given to permit a reversal of the verdict before the actual execution. New evidence was accepted up until the last moment before the execution.

If the accused claimed that he had some new argument in favor of his acquittal, he had to be returned from the field where the execution was to take place to the courtroom as many as four or five times "provided there was something of substance in his words."

The eminent Christian scholar George Foot Moore, commenting on all the laws protecting the accused, concluded: "It is clear that with such a procedure conviction in capital cases was next to impossible, and that this was the intention of the framers of the rules is equally plain."

Decades after the Romans removed from the Sanhedrin the right of imposing capital punishment, several prominent scholars engaged in an academic discussion on capital punishment. Their views, found in Mishna Makkot (1:10), reveals their revulsion against capital punishment even though it had been sanctioned in the past.

A Sanhedrin that puts a man to death once in seven years is called destructive. Rabbi Eleazar ben Azariah says, "Or once in seventy years." Rabbis Tarfon and Akiba said, "If we had been in the Sanhedrin no death sentence would ever have been passed. Rabbi Simeon ben Gamliel said: "If so, they would have multiplied murderers in Israel.

The Talmud asks whether Rabbi Eleazar's statement was a criticism of the old Sanhedrin or whether it described how rare were death sentences. The question is left without a decisive answer. Rabbi Tarfon and Rabbi Akiba probably meant that they would have examined the witnesses so carefully that they would have confused them or caused them to contradict themselves.

Returning to the commandment, "You shall not commit murder," this is the only transgression that is irrevocable. A thief may return the stolen object, pay his fine and ask for forgiveness; a false witness can make amends by admitting his errant conduct. The transgressor may be punished by the court even after he has regretfully acknowledged his wrong, but he may be given another chance to make amends. However, a murderer can never restore the life he has taken away. There is little question that the sixth commandment is the most crucial of the ten, with gravest consequences for the transgressor.

The sin of murder does not originate in the Decalogue, but rather in an early chapter of Genesis. A Midrash states that Cain should have known instinctively that murder was sinful. He could not justly claim that he was unaware of the consequences of his act, that God should have warned him of what could happen to his brother Abel if he were struck down by Cain. No, this is one treacherous deed that a person should be aware of intuitively, requiring no warning or education. Nahum Sarna in his commentary to the Book of Exodus (Jewish Publication Society 1991), reminds the reader that the passage about the first murder mentions the fraternal relationship of Cain to Abel seven times, "a way of indication that all homicide is fratricide." Commenting on God's rebuke to Cain in that text—"Hark, your brother's blood cries out to Me from the ground" (Gen.4:10)—the rabbis in Mishna Sanhedrin (4:5) interpreted the use of the plural form for blood(*demei*) in the Hebrew includes not only the blood of Abel but also the blood of all his potential offspring who would never see the light of day.

Although the commandment against murder is explicit and leaves little room for misunderstanding, many expanded interpretations of this commandment have evolved over time; some seem very appropriate, others more remote. Here is a sampling of interpretations and some misconceptions relating to the sixth commandment:

*Merely the desire to kill another can prove harmful, and should be avoided.* In light of our more recent insights into human behavior, we have learned that many people on occasion have felt like committing murder, but that few follow through with the aggressive act itself; the vengeful thought seldom leads one to take the fateful step, and eventually the thought is dissipated as sanity prevails. Yet, we cannot lightly dismiss the desire to kill as a normal human reaction which eventually passes. A lingering wish to take the life of another human being, whether the target is innocent or not, places the potential victim in harm's way. The raging desire to kill another, if permitted to fester, can end in an irreversible tragedy. We read about these human tragedies regularly: An imaginative plan to take revenge on a competitor who has "stolen" customers and ending up with an obsession to get even, followed by the deliberate act of murder itself. Or the jilted groom who feels that he must kill his competition or the bride who rejected him, and bruised his ego. Feeling the need to revenge the "injustice" may have begun as a simple day-dream; in time, however, the unchecked need to kill would grow into a full-blown passion, followed by a senseless criminal act of murder. The command, "You shall not murder," should be directed not only to the cold criminal mind, but also to the deeply troubled person who feels an intense hatred of a difficult neighbor, a ruthless competitor, an unfaithful spouse.

*Is aborting a fetus regarded as murder?* The claim that any attempt to abort a fetus is a form of murder, regardless of the condition of the fetus or circumstances of the mother's pregnancy, continues to create bitter division in our society. Abortion clinics have been set afire or bombed, physicians' lives have been endangered and even snuffed out by zealots convinced that they are fulfilling God's will by helping to prevent another "murder."

Just about every major religious group has taken a stand on the abortion issue ranging from the ultra conservative view that any tampering with a fetus from the time of conception constitutes murder to the permissive view that the mother can do what she wishes with her own body. Hence, her pregnancy may, therefore, be terminated at any stage before the birth of the child. Most religious groups have taken a position somewhere in between the two extreme views.

Unlike the more stringent Catholic and right-wing Protestant views on abortion, *Judaism does not place abortion in the same category as murder,* the reason being that it is believed life does not begin with conception but at birth. A colleague, Rabbi David Feldman, who has written and lectured extensively on this suject, asserts that the fetus contains potential life, but is not yet a sacred human life.

Some rabbinic authorities are more rigorous than others, permitting abortion only where there was incest or rape or when the mother's life was in jeopardy. Rabbi Feldman reaffirms the traditional Jewish view: "The mother's life takes precedence over that of the unborn child. She has no moral choice when her life is threatened but to abort the fetus; to refuse the procedure is akin to suicide." Other authorities take a more moderate view, sanctioning therapeutic abortion when the mother expresses fear that the infant may be malformed. They reason that priority must be given to the physical and emotional concerns of the mother. Some liberal Jewish authorities will go a step further in sanctioning abortion when the woman accidentally conceives before marriage and refuses to suffer the shame or anguish of producing an unwanted child outside of marriage. Almost all rabbinic authorities, however, discourage abortion on demand, where the woman's health is not in jeopardy, yet she refuses to give birth to a child merely for personal or expedient reasons.

*Is taking one's own life considered an act of murder?* It is not difficult to understand why the traditional Jewish view regarding suicide is uncompromising: Any person who chooses to end his/her life prematurely discards the most precious blessing from God, a-once-in-a-lifetime gift that can never be restored after a suicide. It makes little difference whether someone else destroys that gift or the individual decides to destroy it by his own hand. The result is the same: God's power to bestow life has been rejected by an irrevocable act.

Traditional Jewish law is unequivocal in its harsh judgment against suicide. The Sages creatively included the prohibition against suicide in the seven Noahide laws which were observed before the Ten Commandments were proclaimed to Israel. The body must be buried at the edge of the cemetery, separated from other deceased family members; the survivors are not required to sit *shiva* and recite the traditional mourner's Kaddish. These stringent rulings are meant to serve as a warning, a deterrent against defying the law of God and of nature, no matter how extreme the anguish and pain one has to endure. If Job could hold on to life despite all the personal misfortunes that befell him, should the patient who endures less than the long-suffering Job not choose to cling to life?

However, most rabbinic authorities, with the exception of those who are bound to the stringent interpretation of the law, take a more compassionate view of those who die by their own hand. Naturally, these rabbis would discourage any person from ending his/her own life and would go to great lengths to talk a person out of taking that irreversible step. However, it is generally understood by students of abnormal human behavior that taking one's own life is frequently associated with clinical depression; some people don't have the inner strength to cope with the kind of stress and pressure that others cope with almost routinely in the course of a normal day. Some scientists, though they are not representative of the larger scientific community, contend that the suicidal person carries a defective gene that cannot, as yet, be successfully repaired. Sooner or later the plan to do away with oneself will often be carried out—a compulsion more powerful than the freedom of choice with which most of us are endowed.

Under these unfortunate circumstances when the individual has little or no freedom to choose life, in the presence of extreme existential pain, it would be wrong to judge the tortured soul as one would accuse a murderer. And to deny that person an honorable funeral and burial would show a lack of compassion toward those who are incapable of making a mature decision to choose life in the face of adversity.

Whether suicide is an act of courage or cowardice has long been debated; the question may never be completely resolved. But even with our limited knowledge about the troubled mind that seeks relief from insurmountable problems, Judaism has never looked at this tragic way to find an exit in the same way as it regards the deliberate murder of another person. In sum, taking one's own life is one of several situations that may be termed in Hebrew, *assur aval patur*, a prohibition without penalty, for no one is fully capable of judging the agony of a troubled soul.

*Is assisted suicide a form of murder?* We find many sensitive people praising Doctor Kevorkian as a pathfinder who has taught future generations of physicians how to show compassion for the terminally ill. In spite of having been declared guilty and sent to prison for administering a lethal drug to a dying patient in the presence of millions of viewers on television, Dr. Kevorkian has been declared a hero to many supporters who insist that he is a martyr whose humane view will be accepted by most legislators and by the public in the years to come.

Others are sharply critical of such "merciful acts." They contend that "Dr. Death" is essentially no different than a methodical killer who has irreverently attempted to replace God by shortening the lives of those who lost the desire to continue their struggle with critical illness. They contend that Doctor Kevorkian or his future disciples should be deprived of any further opportunity to be a menace to society.

Although the person who helps the patient end his life is engaged in a form of killing, a reprehensible act, it should not be equated with pre-meditated murder. Assisted suicide does not come under the prohibitions included in the sixth commandment because the patient is asking, even begging for help to terminate his state of misery. Assisted suicide is not a crime of passion based on revenge or bigotry or hatred of another even though it is a seriously misguided act of playing God.

There are circumstances when withholding or withdrawing medications from a patient in a persistent vegetative state may be justified. Such a crucial decision should not be left to the opinion of an individual doctor. Rather a panel of sensitive physicians and ethicists, including clergy, should be able to arrive at an agreement on behalf of the dying patient and his/her family. It goes without saying that the dying patient must have clearly articulated his/her wishes. The committee would be regarded similar to the panel of judges in a court of law, with the added advantage of possessing special knowledge in the fiels of medicine and ethics.*

Can murder ever be justified? If murder is understood as a deliberate and pre-meditated act inspired by random hatred or vengefulness, then it is difficult to find any defense for such a crime. There doesn't seem to be any extenuating circumstances for committing an irrevocable act of murder. And it is this uncompromising prohibition against murder that the sixth commandment addresses.

Jewish tradition is explicit in its claim that only under three exceptional circumstances should a person permit himself to

---

* Generally, I have followed the view of Rabbi Elliot Dorff, Distinguished Professor of Philosophy at the University of Judaism in Los Angeles. His viewe on Jewish medical ethics may be found in his most recent volume, *The Unflolding Tradition*. New York: Aviv Press. Another respected scholar in the area of Jewish medical ethics, Rabbi David Feldman, takes a far more conservative stand than Dorff, based on Feldman's interpretation of the law: "If we knowingly bring about a person's death, we kill ourselves spiritually by having transgressed the boundary between killing and murder." *Where There's Life There's Life*. Brooklyn, N.Y. Yashar Books.

be killed rather than violate the law: If he was under coercion to murder another person, to worship a false god or to engage in incest, which was extended to adultery (B. Sanhedrin 74a). In all other circumstances he may violate a law in order to save his own life.

Confirmed pacifists appear to make no distinction between killing and murder. They will not serve in the armed forces lest they be forced to kill an adversary. They would rather be killed by the enemy than to take another's life. Mahatma Gandhi, a most prominent advocate of pacifism, was consistent in his refusal to bear arms although he was the Indian leader of a successful revolution against British rule. In a 1938 dialogue between Gandhi and Martin Buber, the eminent Jewish philosopher-theologian, Gandhi suggested that the Jews of Germany submit themselves to the Nazis rather than resist their murderous plan to exterminate the Jewish people. He asked that the Jews practice *satyagraha*, soul-force, as an effective form of non-violent resistance to Nazi aggression. The normally gentle Buber rejected Gandhi's advice; he contended that Gandhi did not understand the enormity of the evil the Nazis embodied. Buber understood that Jews could never make a virtue out of self-immolation, national suicide.

*Is the killing of a criminal by the state an act of murder?* The thorny issue of capital punishment will probably continue to be debated into the indefinite future. Does legitimizing capital punishment really deter the potential murderer from taking the fateful step? How many innocent suspects have been executed without positive proof that they had performed the violent act of murder? Now that DNA tests have saved a number of prisoners from execution, is this not a compelling reason to save other prisoners from death row who may have been wrongfully accused?

Why then is the acceptable execution of a criminal by state officials not considered a form of murder in violation of the sixth commandment? Or even if the label of "murder' is not appropriate, why should a court be permitted to execute a convicted criminal where there is a chance that he may be exonerated by new evidence? Is it not preferable to preserve human life even if it entails erring on the side of caution?

The most effective deterrent to the crime of murder is not found in the death chambers of our prisons. Capital punishment may help a grieving family feel that justice was finally done, and thus be able to find some measure of comfort or relief after the brutal death of a relative, but it probably will not discourage a potential murderer who thinks that he can escape the arm of the law without having to pay the ultimate price.

With all the moral and legal problems that capital punishment presents, most Americans still do not care to completely eliminate it, according to the most recent polls. Even those who are comfortable with advocating capital punishment would probably agree that one must not personally take the life of a murderer as an act of revenge. Only the courts, not the individual, may conclude that a death sentence is warranted. The sixth commandment is addressed to the individual, and in the singular: *you* shall not take the life of another person in your hand; if you do so, you are performing an act of murder.

In the spring of 1999 the NATO forces punished the Serbian strategic areas with its most sophisticated weaponry in order to put an end to Serbian brutality in Kosovo. No one will deny that the Kosovars were suffering a miserable fate under a brutal regime in Yugoslavia. A definitive response to the cruel Serbian leadership had to be undertaken. We learned from our bitter past in the Holocaust era that silence in the presence of evil grants permission to tyrants to continue their destructiveness without fear of reprisal.

And yet, we cannot in all good conscience ignore the tragic deaths that befell hundreds of innocent citizens in Yugoslavia who could not be blamed for the ruthless policy of their leaders. Many of these citizens preferred a different government, but were helpless in bringing about any change of leadership. The question begs for an answer: How can we begin to justify the deaths of innocent people even if they were not targeted for death by NATO pilots? Does an apology by a NATO spokesman mitigate the wrong? What is the difference between being mercilessly killed from the air or being shot by a hardened criminal on the streets of Baltimore or New York? Is sanitized bombing from a distance more acceptable, especially if the pilot can't identify the helpless victims or see them writhing in pain? When is killing an invisible victim "merely killing" in a war zone and when is it deemed a cruel act of murder? Can we honestly distinguish between the two kinds of killing, on the street and from the air, and still live within the moral law demanded by the sixth commandment?

The reader may conclude that these questions are being asked by a confirmed pacifist. I have never been comfortable with the uncompromising views that pacifism demands of its adherents. And yet, we must continue to pose these sensitive questions of ourselves and others in order not to lose our perspective about the horrors of war and the sacredness of human life. Waging war must be reserved as a last resort only after other options have been exhausted, such as diplomacy, and even compromise.

Most people who lived through World War II were far less critical of the allied bombing of German cities although the mass destruction resulted in the deaths of hundreds of thousands. The brutal Nazi machine was intent on destroying not only the democratic powers, but also the historic values that have sustained western civilization, based on respect for the value of human life and the dignity of the individual; the whole concept of freedom and democracy that slowly evolved over the centuries was challenged by Hitler's fiendish vision which almost materialized were it not challenged by the full force of allied military power. The deaths suffered by civilians, many of whom were uninvolved in the German military machine, was indeed lamentable. The death of innocent people is always a cause for lament. But we would be hard put to refer to the bombardment of German cities, resulting in many deaths, as an act of genocide or mass murder. There was no other strategic way of weakening the lethal Nazi machine, leading to eventual surrender, without the overwhelming display of allied power.

In our own generation, I cannot quarrel with our government policy to wage war against terrorists who are bent on destroying the lives of Americans on our own soil or in other areas where American citizens must be protected. The same case may be made in defense of Israel's armed forces who have been forced to wage war against terrorism. So long as these terrorist organizations refuse to accept Israel's legitimate existence in the Middle East, a peaceful solution cannot be achieved.

The ancient religious principle found in Genesis that every person is created in God's image carries a powerful message for those who are receptive to its meaning. When we consciously take another person's life, we deny God's pervasive role in our lives; we challenge God's authority in the world. However, when we are able to save a life from a premature death, we enhance God's image in the world and we reaffirm God's authority and influence in our lives. We pay the ultimate tribute to the God of all humanity.

# Insights From The Sages

## No Justification for Murder

A man came to Raba and said: "The prefect in my town has ordered me to kill another person, or he will kill me." Raba replied: "Let him kill you; you must not commit murder. Why should you think your blood is redder than his? Perhaps his is redder than yours!"

(Pesahim 25b)

## To Bring about Healing, One May Violate Any Precept Except those Prohibiting Idolatry, Unchastity, and Murder

What is the proof that one may not violate the prohibition against murder? If a man were told, "Go slay this person and you will be healed," he must not follow such advice, for it is written, "Whoever sheds the blood of man, by man shall his blood be shed" (Gen. 9:6). Now since a man who sheds blood must have his own blood shed, how can one who is ill be healed by the shedding of blood?

(Exodus Rabbah 16:2)

## Greed Can Lead to Murder

"Cain said to Abel his brother" (Gen. 4:8). What Cain said to Abel was: "Come let us divide the world between us." Abel agreed. So Cain said: "You take the chattel, and I will take the land." And it was agreed between them that neither should have any claim against the other about the division. Nevertheless, when Abel proceeded to graze the flock, Cain said: "The land you are standing on is mine!" Abel replied: "The clothing you are wearing belongs to me!" Abel said: "Take off!" Cain said: "Get off!" At that, "Cain rose up against Abel his brother" (Gen.4:8).

(Genesis Rabbah 22:7)

## God Is Blamed for Permitting Murder

"The voice of your brother's blood cries out *against Me* from the ground" (Gen 4:10). [Instead of "unto Me" the word *eilai* may be read here *alay*—against Me]. Rabbi Shimon bar Yohai commented: This verse is difficult to recite and impossible to explain. It seems to regard Cain and Abel like two gladiators wrestling in the king's presence. If the king wishes, he may separate them, or if he does not wish to separate them, and one gladiator prevails over the other and is about to kill him, the other may cry out, "Who will intercede for me before the king?" [Therefore, God said: Since I, the King, did not interfere between Cain and Abel] "The voice of your brother's blood cries out *against* Me."

(Genesis Rabbah 22:9)

## Repentance: The Beginning of Rehabilitation

Cain asked: "Is my sin so great that it cannot be borne? You bear the whole world, yet my sin you cannot bear?" God replied to him, "Since you have repented [by admitting your sinful act], go forth from here as a wandering exile."And Cain went out from the Lord's presence and dwelled as a wanderer in the land (Gen. 4:16).

(Tanhuma Beresheet 25)

לֹא תִּנְאָף.

You shall not commit adultery.

# Seventh Commandment

# Reflections

The prohibition against adultery is mentioned explicitly for the first time in the Decalogue. Yet, according to a well-known rabbinic tradition, seven basic rules were commanded to the sons of Noah long before the Torah was given at Sinai, including the prohibition against sexual transgressions, such as adultery and incest. At a later period when the Jews governed themselves, these Noahide laws were designed to be a standard for all non-Jews living within the Jewish community. Although they were not required to observe the ritual commandments, such as the Sabbath or circumcision, they were expected to remain faithful to their partners in marriage, just as they were required to guard themselves against the sin of theft, bloodshed, blasphemy, etc.

It was apparent to the religious authorities that the Jewish community could not permit licentiousness among one segment of the population, and at the same time, require marital faithfulness among Jews. That same reasoning accounts for the law against bigamy in the United States; the law could not tolerate a special law for those Mormons who contend that bigamy should be sanctioned even though their religion permitted it, and another law requiring monogamy for the rest of the citizens. Yemenite Jews as well who migrated to Israel in the early fifties, were no longer permitted to follow the Muslim tradition of marrying as many as four wives. They were permitted to keep the wives they had already married, but not add to them. Some of the long-standing traditions practiced by Jews who once lived in Muslim countries had to be discarded in order to avoid a double standard among neighboring ethnic groups in Israel.

The biblical law against adultery is more complex than appears on the surface. The Torah's definition of adultery applies only to a married woman who has a sexual relationship with a man other than her husband. The Torah does not explicitly forbid a married man from having a sexual encounter, even a prolonged relationship with another woman, so long as she is unmarried. Jacob, for example, had two wives and two concubines. David and Solomon both had multiple wives. King David sinned by taking a married woman, Bathsheba, into his harem. King Solomon's marriage to many foreign women, bringing into his palace alien religious beliefs and practices, jeopardized the perpetuation of monotheism. Solomon was unable to resist the blandishments of his foreign wives.

Since biblical society was essentially patriarchal, with the husband having exclusive rights to the women in his household, she was required, under severe penalties, to be faithful to him.

In the Bible, the punishment for adultery is death, and without the opportunity to ask for or to extend forgiveness. Even after capital punishment was almost abolished in the first century, the authorities continued to maintain that an adulterous woman was forbidden to both her husband and to her lover.

It is of interest to note that, in ancient Judaism, polygamy was not explicitly forbidden. If marriage to more than one wife was solemnized, neither the man nor his wives were regarded as adulterers.

Nevertheless, as far back as patriarchal times, monogamy seemed to be preferable to polygamy. Abraham brought Hagar into his household because his wife Sarah couldn't produce a descendant in her normal childbearing years in order to guarantee continuity. Isaac was born in Abraham and Sarah's old age. Isaac had only one wife. Jacob preferred Rachel as his only wife but was tricked into taking Leah, the elder sister, before marrying Rachel. Joseph married one wife. The Bible doesn't clearly indicate that Moses was married to two wives simultaneously. The very opening of Genesis seems to express the ideal marital condition when it directs the man to leave his mother and father and cleave unto his wife (2:24).

What is noteworthy is that we do not have a record of any rabbinic authority mentioned in the Talmud who was married to more than one wife, even though polygamy was not explicitly prohibited at that time. Not until the beginning of the eleventh century was polygamy forbidden by the prominent rabbinic leader Rabbenu Gershom, and his edict applied only to the Ashkenazic community, and not to Sephardic Jewry, which was unrestricted by his authority. Rabbenu Gershom's ban on polygamy seemed to imply that anyone who was married to more than one wife after the announcement of his ban was guilty of an adulterous relationship.

The seventh commandment along with the rest of the Decalogue continues to be read publicly in the synagogue three times in the year: during the Torah reading found in the Books of Exodus and Deuteronomy, and on the holiday of Shavuot. Hardly anyone would be so bold as to seriously suggest that the Torah reader recite the two words forbidding adultery in an undertone or skip over the commandment entirely. And yet, many enlightened people, even those who themselves have been faithful to one partner throughout their marriage, try to find some justification for infidelity among their family members or friends. Even the use of the word "adultery" sounds archaic and excessively judgmental to some who take pride in their sophistication.

We should ask ourselves with all candor whether the seventh commandment is still relevant, especially since it is treated so casually and usually without either party having to suffer punishment in the eyes of the law. Some people have seriously suggested that the biblical prohibition should be "kept on the books" as an ideal, like some of our civil laws which have never been removed from the statutes, yet are never enforced when they are broken.

A growing segment of the population would agree that adultery can no longer be regarded as a punishable prohibition, especially if two consenting adults are engaged in the act. They are in charge of their personal behavior and hopefully aware of the consequences of their action. Moreover, if they do not reveal their little secret to anyone else, they will not cause harm to their respective partners or their children. In fact, they may believe that they can enhance their marriage by engaging occasionally in an extra-marital affair; they return to their spouses with a greater appreciation for those redeeming virtues which extend beyond sexual attraction.

Others will agree that engaging in extra-marital sex constitutes an indiscretion, if not a religious transgression, but can, nevertheless, be justified in extenuating circumstances. "My wife shows no interest in sex, neither in finding sexual satisfaction for herself nor in satisfying my needs." "My husband has no clue as to what really pleases a woman. He doesn't care to know how men and women are aroused differently."

There is, to be sure, any number of rationalizations for engaging in an adulterous relationship. The need to justify an extra-marital relationship to oneself or to others can appear more reasonable than to admit that a wrong is being committed in finding sex outside of marriage. *But attempting to find justification does not address the basic moral problem.* To violate a trust, to abrogate a vow made at the time of marriage, cannot be justified whether the offended partner is or is not aware of what has transpired. A marital bond has been severed; mutual trust has been compromised. It makes little difference whether we choose to call a sexual relationship outside marriage a sinful activity, an indiscretion, or a self-indulgent act. However adultery may be described or rationalized, the results can be most unfortunate. Innocent people are hurt; complete trust is seldom fully restored.

I recall a situation involving personal friends which could possibly be considered an exceptional condition allowing for an adulterous relationship. A young woman was stricken with an incurable nerve condition two years after marriage. Her speech and mind were not affected by her condition but otherwise her body was left totally inert. After several years of unsuccessful surgery and therapy, she told her doting husband that she wouldn't want to grant him a divorce, which would cause her to give up her struggle to survive, yet, she would encourage him to find his sexual gratification with another woman. Initially, he refused to accept her offer, but subsequently changed his mind, knowing that he had received her encouragement to look elsewhere for his sexual needs. The husband abandoned her after several months. She succumbed soon after.

The many friends of the couple were deeply saddened by the woman's death. The common reaction was that she died of a broken heart. Yet, they did not fault the husband for entering into another relationship outside of marriage. He followed the advice of his invalid wife, who wanted her husband to continue to enjoy some physical pleasure. The friends' only complaint against him was that he abandoned her when he could have continued to give her the attention that she required and deserved. Can anyone be surprised at the outcome of this permissive arrangement?

We should be aware that adultery, even with consent, constitutes a clear violation of the seventh commandment. For example, we are aware of couples who continue to live under the same roof, and yet have a consensual arrangement to find their sexual fulfillment with other partners outside the home. They claim, for example, that as long as the permission given to each other is mutual, neither partner is hurt in the process. Or they will assert that so long as their children continue to see both parents together at home on weekends and holidays, then they need not feel any apprehension about their unconventional lifestyle. Yet, granting mutual consent in itself should not be understood as a sanction to act out one's fantasy. An adulterous relationship may not have the same serious repercussions in the public eye as it once had, but the effect on the contemporary family can prove no less devastating. The emotional needs of the children, whatever their ages, have not basically changed over the years even though the sexual mores of former generations were far more restrictive.

In sum, few people register surprise any longer when they read or hear about policy-makers or entertainers or even neighbors for whom the seventh commandment is merely a helpful suggestion, not a moral imperative. Even many men and women who themselves have been faithful to their partners throughout marriage, choose not to be critical of their friends who remain less faithful than themselves. That is why President Bill Clinton continued to maintain his popularity with the American public in spite of his widely-publicized sexual indiscretions. The majority of Americans continued to support its flawed but charismatic leader; they were only mildly upset by his infidelity; they were less tolerant of his denying and lying about his intimate relationships. It stands to reason, however, that if many seem to have outgrown the importance of the seventh commandment, then the continued influence of religious values in the future will have been seriously impaired.

# Insights From The Sages

## Adultery Starts With The Heart

". . .So that you do not follow your heart and eyes in your lustful urge" (Num. 15:39). From this verse it follows, said Rabbi [Judah, the Prince], that one should not drink out of one goblet while thinking of another.

(B. Nedarim 20b)

## Respecting Each Family's Right To Privacy

"And Balaam looked up and saw Israel encamped tribe by tribe so that he was impelled to exclaim, `The spirit of God should rest upon Israel'" (Num.24:2). What did Balaam see? He saw that the entrances to Israel's tents did not face one another [so as to ensure privacy]. So he exclaimed, "These people deserve to have the Divine Presence rest upon them."

(B. Baba Batra 60a)

## The Greater the Person, the Stronger His Urge

Abbaya, hearing a man say to a woman, "Let us arise early and go on our way," said to himself: I will follow them to prevent them from doing what is prohibited. He followed them through meadows a distance of three parasangs. As they were about to separate, he heard them say, "The company is pleasant but the way is long." Abbaya said: If I were in their place, I could not have restrained myself. In deep anguish he leaned against the bolt in a doorway. An elder appeared and recited the tradition: "The greater the man, the stronger his impulse to do evil."

(B. Sukkah 52a)

לֹא תִּגְנֹב.

You shall not steal.

# Eighth Commandment

# Reflections

Perhaps it is no accident that the prohibition against stealing is mentioned immediately after the seventh commandment prohibiting adultery. Isn't the adulterous act a form of theft, snatching away the feelings of loyalty and commitment from a legitimate partner, now sharing these feelings with an unlawful party! Stealth and deception are usually present in the mind of the thief just as one often finds in an illicit relationship. Whether the positioning of the two adjacent commandments was deliberate we cannot be at all certain, but it does have pedagogic value for those who view these two commandments with a sense of serious concern.

The commandment against stealing refers to taking any object from another person without his\her consent. Even borrowing an object or a sum of money with the intention of returning it at a later date is regarded as theft as long as the owner is unaware that his possession has been removed. The rabbis extend the prohibition to those who "steal" an object as a practical joke or just to annoy one's neighbor without any intention of keeping it permanently. Another's possessions should never be dealt with casually.

Some authorities contend that the main thrust of the eighth commandment was originally directed against stealing another person—kidnapping or man-stealing, which was a capital of-

fense. Stealing an object from another, as serious as it is regarded in the Torah, requires the thief to compensate the victim by paying double the value of the stolen object. The penalty was greater for stealing domestic animals. There were no
jails in which to lock up thieves, but kidnapping was seen as a
sin in a class with murder.

Nahum Sarna clarifies the crime of kidnapping in his commentary on the Book of Exodus (Jewish Publication Society,
p. 123). He asserts that the main motive for kidnapping was to
coerce the victim into servitude, either to the kidnapper himself or to another master who was willing to pay a price for the
human merchandise.

It is a reasonable assumption then that this commandment
was primarily directed against body-snatching and not the lesser
crime of stealing a material object. The law against kidnapping
is re-iterated in Exodus 21:16 which states, "He who kidnaps a
man—whether he has sold him or is still holding him—shall be
put to death.". Some rabbinic authorities felt that this commandment dealt exclusively with the sin of kidnapping, and the
stealing of objects was covered by the last commandment: "You
shall not covet." Their reasoning was that when an individual
covets another person's possession, he would naturally be en-
ticed to steal it. Coveting, then, is the first step to the criminal
act of stealing. Although this rabbinic view appears logical, the
weight of scholarly opinion does not support it. The commandment against stealing probably refers to both the unlawful re-
moval of material things *and* kidnapping; even though the punishment for the former is merely monetary, the latter involves
capital punishment.

Jewish law has much to say about thievery. For example, a
distinction is made between robbery and theft. The thief who
secretly intrudes during the night must pay as his fine double
the value of the property stolen; the brazen robber who commits his crime openly simply makes restitution to the owner of
the stolen property. Theft was considered more serious because the stealthy thief fears the punishment of men but not
the judgment of God. "He honors the servant more than the
Master." The robber, however, treats the servant equally with

the Master—he respects neither. Therefore, the person who shows greater respect for the authority of man than for God's authority commits the greater wrong and is more severely punished (B. Bava Kamma 79b).

The Sages concern themselves with more than the moral problem of restoring stolen property. The offender was also expected to seek forgiveness of the person whom he exploited. Only after showing genuine remorse does God forgive the thief. Commenting on the verse, "He shall restore that which he took by robbery," the rabbis derive the moral lesson that things taken by force cannot be acquired legally even when full payment of their worth is made to the owner. Only if stolen property is destroyed does the robber return the full value of the object; if it still exists, the stolen object must be returned. It stands to reason that the owner may have an emotional attachment to the object illicitly taken from him—an heirloom or an inheritance passed on from parents or grandparents. He will not be satisfied to accept a substitute or a monetary settlement. Moreover, even after returning the stolen object, the robber must ask forgiveness of his victim because he violated a basic command found in the Torah.

The rabbis expanded the prohibition against stealing to include two other moral issues. The first dealt with the need to return a lost object to its legitimate owner. The old saw, "Finders keepers, losers weepers," is regarded as an alien concept both in the biblical and talmudic code of behavior. Even if no reward were offered by the owner of the lost object, so long as the finder was able to identify the owner, there was no question about the urgent necessity of returning it. The failure to return a lost object was no less serious than outright theft.

The Torah extends the command of returning lost property by asserting that it makes no difference whether the lost object belongs to a friend or an adversary. The object must be returned or it becomes "hot property." The verse in Exodus (23:4) clearly sets the rule: "When you encounter your enemy's ox or ass wandering, you must take it back to him." Although the hope exists that the owner of the animal will be appreciative of the gesture made by the finder and will eventually be converted into a friend, returning the animal is not contingent on the possibility of an amicable outcome. Even if the finder and the loser cannot reconcile their former differences, the restoration of the animal has to be made to prevent a theft. Here we have a classical example in which a passive act—doing nothing—can result in a tangible violation of the eighth commandment.

The second derivative lesson included in the prohibition against theft is found in the rabbinic concept called *genevat daat*, stealing another's mind, i.e., deception. To create a false impression is no less serious than the physical act of removing another's possession to one's own domain. Maimonides expands on the talmudic law against deception with the exhortation: "It is forbidden to cheat people in trade or to deceive them. This same rule applies to both Jew and non-Jew. He who knows there is a defect in his wares is required to notify the purchaser."

*Genevat daat* does not apply exclusively to business dealings. The deceitful person may be scrupulous in his business dealings and yet "steal the heart" of his neighbor in a social setting. Rabbi Meir used to say: "A man should not urge his friend to dine with him if he knows that his friend will not do so. Nor should he offer him any gifts if he knows that his friend will not accept them. He should not make believe that it is for his guest's sake that he is opening casks of wine that, in fact, he intends to turn over to a shopkeeper to be sold; he must inform his guest what his true intentions are" (B. Hulin 94a).

The Sages have much to say on the matter of honesty in business. Both buyer and seller are required to adopt a personal code of honesty and to demand it of the other party. Where there is willful deceit or misunderstanding, either party may cancel the transaction, even after it was already consummated. Much attention was given to the accuracy of weights and measures. "A wholesaler must clean out his measures monthly and a householder once a year. Rabbi Simeon ben Gamliel says that the contrary is the rule. The shopkeeper must clean out his measure twice a week, polish his weights weekly, and clean out his scales after every weighing."

Just as the seller must be honest with the purchaser, so must the potential buyer be straightforward with the seller. "One should not say, 'How much is this item?' if he has no intention to buy it." Although this view may sound a bit naive and unrealistic to most people, the reasoning is morally sound. The deliberate wasting of a businessman's valuable time, possibly taking him away from a "live customer," was regarded as a form of thievery—stealing precious time from the seller and falsely raising his hopes.

In today's complex business world we find *genevat daat* prevalent in various areas. The advertisement industry has been harshly, but justly criticized for misrepresenting the true value of its products. Appliances and cars are occasionally "dressed up" to look better than they really are; packaged goods are attractively wrapped and sold almost exclusively on eye appeal; customers are deceived into believing that they are getting bargains at discount stores when they are really offered inferior merchandise or "discounts" from a fictitious price. These and other practices have long been tolerated if not encouraged in the name of healthy competition that turns the wheels of our capitalist system. Only in recent years have government agencies become more aggressive by stepping in to investigate these fraudulent claims, especially in the advertisement field.

To be sure, the warnings against deception articulated in the rabbinic literature were directed to a less complex business community than today. But the need to protect innocent consumers from fraud and deception—the attempt to "steal one's mind"—remains a major problem today that urgently needs to be aggressively addressed  by vigilant government agencies.

Rabbi Bernard Zlotowitz, senior scholar at the Union of American Hebrew Congregations, wisely suggested to me that to engage in plagiarism, the appropriation of another person's ideas or language and representing the material as one's original work, is a form of deception—*genevat daat*. In recent years we have heard about a growing number of journalists, celebrated writers and gifted scholars who were found to have lifted whole passages in their works without attribution.

Although the public may not regard the "plague of plagiarism" as a significant offense compared to some of the major moral infractions committed in the commercial world, the effect is far more serious than we are aware of. Plagiarism involves two offenses: Theft (*genevah*) and deception (*genevat daat*). On the one hand, the plagiarist takes a thought or idea from another without permission and claims it to be his own. It makes little difference whether he takes a tangible object or claims posession or an idea. The act is basically the same.

The second infraction, deception, is also apparent. The plagiarist wishes the reader or student to think that he, and not the original author, gave birth to the idea. He wishes to receive the credit at the expense of the person who deserves the public approval.

The Talmud Sanhedrin (25b) distinguishes between two kinds of robbers—a robber in the biblical sense and the robber mentioned in a wider rabbinical sense. The former is one who illegally seizes the property of another by force or intimidation. The latter, called *gazlan derabanan*, is interpreted as a professional gambler, a person of questionable character and credibility, who is not permitted to serve as a witness in court. The Sages were severe in their assessment of the professional gambler. He earns his living at the expense of vulnerable people who were led to believe that they could invest little and earn much. The professional gambler is liable on two counts: he takes money that doesn't rightfully belong to him and he "steals one's mind" by holding out false hopes that the victim can fulfill his dream of becoming an instant winner, or that he has a fair chance to win against the professional.

It is understandable why stealing has never gone out of style in spite of warnings against theft found in ancient sacred texts. Even the threat of punishment from parents and other authorities for stealing has not eliminated the temptation to steal. The rationalizations are easily formulated, and the guilty conscience can be quickly assuaged. "The big companies are so rich and powerful; if I get on the bus without having to pay, no one will ever miss my fare." "Pilferage is built into the company's business expense, its cost of doing business." "They give their employees reason to take a little here and there; they have never paid their dedicated workers a decent living wage. We must look out for ourselves. We have our families to feed."

It should be self-evident that exploitation and greed practiced by several giant corporations, no matter how reprehensible, cannot justify taking the law into our own hands to get even or to resist exploitation. Jewish law clearly repudiates the action of one who is *gonev mi-ganav,* the person who steals from a thief. The transgressor is required to make restitution by returning the principle even to an unsavory character, the lesson being that we must preserve our personal integrity at all costs.

The simple and direct warning against theft found in the Decalogue could not possibly have anticipated the exploitation of employees who confidently planned for their retirement after faithfully serving Enron or World Com. To their dismay, they were notified that their long anticipated golden years in retirement had come to an abrupt end with little or nothing to show for all their years of planning.

It was not until their employers were exposed that the employees fully realized what had happened to them: They became victims of theft, sophisticated schemes, complex transactions that only the few knew of or could comprehend, but which left thousands of people, employees and investors, bereft of funds that rightfully belonged to them.

Should there be any difference in the way a common thief who breaks into a convenience store is apprehended and the executive who steals from the company at the expense of the employees? Should the executive serve less time because he can afford the most clever legal advisers to defend him or should the damage done to the lives of hundreds or thousands be considered first and foremost in considering the punishment of these moguls? In sum, should sophisticated stealing from the public be treated with less severity by the courts than the act of simply stealing an animal or object from one's neighbor as it was originally envisioned in the Decalogue?

On the one hand, corporate theft is more dramatic, requiring elaborate planning than simple theft of a neighbor's object. Because of the complexity of modern corporate crime, it may take months, even years, to unravel the extent of the damage done to the employees or investors. However, regardless of the size of the theft, the effect of petty or corporate thievery is basically the same: the thief dares to take something that he has not honestly earned; the victims must depend on a just legal system to retrieve what rightfully belongs to them, often without a successful outcome. Whatever the nature of the crime, the eighth commandment is unambiguous and needs little elaboration to be understood by both the perpetrator or the victim.

The commandment against stealing is addressed not only to hardened criminals or kleptomaniacs; it is also directed to ordinary citizens who have no record of being reprimanded for theft, but who nevertheless need to be cautioned that no one is immune from the temptation to steal.

Although Jewish law condemns the thief and finds no justification for plying his trade, a few Hasidic masters playfully comment on the personality of the thief as a helpful teacher to the masses.

The Great Maggid exclaimed to Rabbi Zusya, his disciple: "I cannot teach you the ten principles on how one can serve his Creator, but you may learn three things from a little child and seven things from a thief. From the child we learn that he is merry for no particular reason; he is constantly busy; when he wants something he demands it vigorously.

"From the thief we may learn that he does his service by night; what he doesn't obtain in one night, he will devote the next night to it; he and his fellow workers are loyal to one another; he risks his life for slight gains; what he takes has so little value to him that he gives it up for a pittance; he endures blows and hardship, and it matters nothing to him; nothing can induce him to change his trade, meaning that he does not want to be anyone but himself." (Adapted from *Ten Rungs* by Martin Buber, p. 55.)

It is apparent that the Maggid's humorous yet profound observations on the personality of the thief was meant to teach that, if we are wise, we should be able to learn from everyone—even from those who are a threat to society. Furthermore, God is unhappy with the life that the thief has chosen, but He does not totally reject any of His children, even those who have estranged themselves from God.

# Insights From The Sages

## Means and Ends Should Both Be Honorable

We have been taught that Rabbi Eliezer ben Jacob said: "He who steals a *seah* of wheat, grinds it, kneads it into dough, bakes it, and even sets aside a portion as *hallah*—what blessing could he possibly utter? Surely he may not utter a blessing, for he would be blaspheming, as is said, 'The robber who utters a blessing blasphemes the Lord'" (Ps. 10:3).

(B.Bava Kamma 94a)

## The Thief Cares Only for His Own Needs

Mar Zutra the Pious once had a silver cup stolen from him at an inn. When he saw one disciple wash his hands and wipe them on another disciple's garments, he exclaimed, "That is the one, since he has no regard for his fellow's property." The disciple was put in fetters, and then he confessed.

(B. Bava Metzia 24a)

## The Receiver of Stolen Goods Is Worse Than the Thief

There is a tale about a ruler who would put to death receivers of stolen property but let the thieves go. Everyone criticized him for not acting rationally. So what did he do? He had it proclaimed throughout his province, "All people to the arena!" Next, what did he do? He brought weasels and placed before them portions of food. The weasels took the portions and carried them to their holes.

The following day, he again had it proclaimed, "Everyone to the arena!" Again he brought weasels and placed before them portions of food, but this time he sealed the holes, so that when the weasels took their food to the holes and found them stopped up, they returned the portions to where they had been.

Thus they demonstrated that, but for receivers, there would be no thievery.

(Leviticus Rabbah 6:2)

## One Who Steals from a Gentile Will Come to Steal From a Jew

The Torah was given only to hallow God's great Name, as it is said, "God said to me: `You are My servant, Israel, through whom I will be glorified' " (Is.49:3). [By your deeds, you will glorify Me among all men]. Hence, the Sages said, a man should keep away from dishonesty in dealing, whether with a Jew or Gentile, indeed, with anyone in the marketplace. Besides, he who steals from a Gentile will in the end steal from a Jew; he who cheats a Gentile will in the end cheat a Jew; he who swears [falsely] to a Gentile will in the end swear [falsely] to a Jew; he who acts deceitfully toward a Gentile will eventually act deceitfully toward a Jew; he who sheds the blood of a Gentile will in the end, shed the blood of a Jew.

(Tanna De-bei Eliyahu, ed. Friedmann, p.140; JPS p. 347)

לֹא תַעֲנֶה בְרֵעֲךָ
עֵד שָׁקֶר.

You shall not bear false
witness against your neighbor.

# Ninth Commandment

# Reflections

I have found it difficult to explain to students that the ninth commandment should be read with the same emphasis and sense of urgency as the three previous commands, the admonition against murder, adultery and theft. To lie in a court of law is a serious matter, to be sure, but it doesn't appear, on the surface at least, to be in the same league with the previous infractions. In fact, very few biblical commentaries devote much space to the gravity of the ninth commandment.

Some background is necessary to properly understand why the ninth command has earned an essential place in the Decalogue. To this very day witnesses play a crucial role in the judicial process. This reliance on credible witnesses was just as important in the biblical era. Just as today, so in the ancient world false evidence offered by dishonorable witnesses would obstruct the administration of justice and threaten public confidence in the integrity of the courts. This could cause the collapse of the rule of law. That is why firm steps were needed to discourage false testimony in the court: Two or more witnesses were required for evidence to be accepted; false witnesses were given the same punishment that would have been imposed on the accused, including capital punishment. In sum, witnesses, like judges, acted as God's representatives or surrogates here on earth. When a witness deliberately presented false testimony, he denied God's role as the ultimate champion of justice.

The question arose whether the commandment against bearing false witness applied to the treatment of one Israelite to another or did the prohibition also apply to the treatment of any person. The use of the Hebrew term *re-ah*, neighbor or friend, found in the ninth commandment, occasionally refers to a fellow Jew. However, there are times when *re-ah* includes non-Israelites as well, as we find in Exodus 11:2, "Tell the people that each man shall borrow from his neighbor, and each woman from hers, objects of silver and gold." It is obvious from this verse that "neighbor" refers to the Egyptians—to any human being. Hence, the commandment against giving false testimony applies to any and all members of the community. To apply this commandment only to another Jew would appear to be as serious a transgression as a violation of the commandment itself.

The prohibition against delivering false testimony, an essential value in the Jewish system of ethics and justice, is not meant to include telling the truth under all conditions and at any cost. The German philosopher Immanuel Kant was known to take an uncompromising view on the subject of truth-telling. He went so far as to permit the killing of a fellow human rather than lie to a potential murderer. Kant reasoned that the person who divulged the truth of the victim's whereabouts need not feel guilt. If one tells the truth, he cannot, strictly speaking, be responsible for the murder that another person commits. The murderer must assume the entire blame for his act. In speaking the truth, he has done nothing worthy of blame. If, on the other hand, one tells the intended murderer a lie, he becomes responsible for all the bad consequences which could happen to the victim. For example, one may point the murderer in what one believes to be the wrong direction, only to discover that that is exactly where the victim went into hiding. This uncompromising view on the immorality of lying is rejected by most moralists, who contend that under special circumstances a lie is justifiable, especially when innocent lives are at stake, and where only an untruth can prevent human tragedy from happening.

In the rich rabbinic literature much emphasis is placed on the essential value of avoiding falsehood. The world, we are told, rests on the three-fold principles of truth, justice and peace. The Hebrew word for truth, *emet*, consists of the first, middle and last letters of the Hebrew alphabet to instruct us that truth should pervade all of life.

Yet, there are times when the pursuit of peace takes priority over truth in our hierarchy of values. A familiar midrash serves to remind us that even God tells an untruth in the Bible. God reports to Sarah that she will give birth to a son. Sarah laughs, and replies, "How can I give birth, my husband is too old!" But God, in reporting the conversation to Abraham, tells him, "Your wife laughed saying *she* is too old." The rabbis comment that God told this untruth in order to prevent conflict between Abraham and Sarah. They learn from this incident that it is permitted to tell a white lie in order to promote *shelom bayit*, peace in the household. Another citation: The High Priest Aaron, a pursuer of peace, was known to tell a white lie in order to bring two erstwhile friends together once again. He would report to each one that the other regretted the friction that occurred between them. Aaron's white lie was justified for the greater cause of restoring peace between neighbors.

The Talmud relates three exceptions to the rule of truthfulness: "tractate," "bed," and "hospitality." "Tractate" is explained to mean that if a scholar is asked if he is familiar with a portion of the Talmud, out of modesty, he may untruthfully claim that he is ignorant of the passage. An untruth is permitted to avoid giving the appearance of arrogance. "Bed" is explained by the master Biblical and Talmudic commentator Rashi to mean that if a scholar is questioned about his marital relations he may resort to an untruthful answer. We can assume that the scholar is encouraged here to minimize his virility when another party questions him about his sexual performance. "Hospitality" means that a scholar who has been treated well by his host can decide not to reveal the truth about his reception if he is concerned that his host may be embarrassed by a flood of unwelcome guests.

Although the ninth commandment is explicit, it implies more

than giving false testimony in court. The rabbis extend the meaning of the commandment to include *leshon ha-ra*, literally an evil tongue, which covers a wide range of abusive speech, *whether true or false*. Maimonides defines *leshon ha-ra* in this way: A person with a malicious tongue is one who, sitting in company, says, "That person did such a thing; his ancestors were so and so; I have heard this about him;" and then he proceeds to disgrace him.

There are other forms of *leshon ha-ra* that are camouflaged, but nevertheless deplored because they result in character defamation. When one opens a conversation saying, "I do not want to discuss what happened to an individual," he may be trying to arouse the curiosity of the listener, and in his own way plant seeds of suspicion although not accusing anyone outright.

Broadly speaking *leshon ha-ra* may include the following verbal infractions, or "diseases of the mouth": Mocking or ridiculing another person; slanderous speech, which always carries malicious intent; gossip which may be malicious or just playful, but nevertheless harmful; shaming another person in public, for which there is no effective repentance; defaming another's good reputation in order to elevate himself above the accused.

*Ridicule*: The rabbis vehemently criticize the person who speaks disparagingly of a convert to Judaism, reminding others of the convert's non-Jewish origin. A convert to the Jewish faith is to be treated no less respectfully than a Jew by birth. Some authorities contend that the Jew by choice, because of his/her courageous decision, should be shown even greater respect than the native-born Jew. One authority goes so far as to claim that the Biblical personality Ruth, who freely chose to accept the Jewish faith, performed an heroic act as momentous as the giving of the Torah at Sinai—one of the reasons suggested for reading the Book of Ruth on the holiday of Shavuot, when the giving of the Torah is commemorated.

*Slanderous speech*: There is no way to adequately defend oneself against spreading false information. Half truths are frequently more difficult to defend than outright lies.

*Gossip*: The Torah is explicit about the destructiveness of gossip: "You shall not go about as a talebearer among your fellows" (Lev.19:16). One may think that gossip is confined to the poorly educated social class who have little else to do with their time than to spin tales of gossip about others. However, gossip pervades all strata of society. Even some scholars who issue lofty pronouncements on the evils of gossip are not immune from the very practices they tend to criticize.

It is noteworthy that of all the transgressions, gossip is perhaps the easiest to engage in. The great satisfaction derived from gossip, by the speaker (or writer) and the listener (or reader), is immediately felt; usually there is no legal penalty to deter gossip. Thus the temptation is maximal, and the guilt feelings minimal, especially when the gossip is true. And yet, the Sages remind us that those transgressions such as talebearing that are easiest to commit should not be regarded as trivial. On the contrary, the damage, though usually imperceptible, can be more destructive than those major infractions rarely performed by the general public.

There is yet another kind of gossip that is least perceptible, which is why it is given the curious name: "dust of gossip" (*avak rekhilut*). The highly regarded medieval commentator Rashi defines a "dust of gossip" in this way: "Someone asks of another, `Where can I find fire?' and the other replies, `Fire may be found in the house of so and so where there is an abundance of meat and fish, and where they are always cooking something.' By adding the words, `They are always cooking something,' he is spreading 'dust of gossip,' implying that they are always feasting there."

*Shaming another in public*: Of all the verbal transgressions mentioned in rabbinic literature, the Sages are most highly critical of the person who embarrasses another in a public place. Here is a sampling of their reaction to such insensitivity: A person who profanes the sacred, despises the Festivals, *shames others publicly*, annuls the covenant of our patriarch Abraham, and contemptuously perverts the meaning of Torah. Though steeped in learning and the performance of good deeds, they shall have no share in the world-to-come" (Pirkei Avot

3:15).

"It is preferable to hurl oneself into a fiery furnace rather than shame another person in public" (Berakhot 47b).

A tanna recited before Nahman b. Isaac: "He who publicly shames his neighbor is regarded as though he shed blood" (Bava Metzia 58b).

Why is there no effective repentance for shaming another in public even when the aggressor is remorseful? Because he is unable to reach all the people who originally heard his humiliating remark in public and then attempt to express his regrets to them individually.

*Defaming another's good reputation*: Although defamation of character may technically be subsumed under gossip or slander, it deserves to be mentioned independently because it is so widely practiced and accepted without reservation, especially in the political arena. A candidate for political office cannot be effective, so we are advised, unless he can verbally wound his opponent so it will damage his credibility. He must find ways to plant suspicion about his/her social habits, sexual indiscretions, reckless spending, etc. The really substantive issues of the political campaign are often tangential; the personal issues can and often do determine the outcome of a political campaign.

What should disturb sensitive people is that character defamation—*leshon ha-ra*—is regarded as acceptable practice and even identified with the democratic process, a legitimate manifestation of free speech. There is no way to enforce civility in speech, unless it is clearly libel or slander. No one wishes to muzzle the candidates for office. Yet, the public should demand fewer vitriolic attacks against a patriotic citizen who aspires to public office. Fewer and fewer people with exceptional ability and stature choose to run for office precisely because they will not want to endure the ordeal of character assassination by one's opponent or by the media. Political parties must come to grips with the need for radical change in the way they treat political opponents during the heat of a campaign. The public, the ultimate consumer, should indicate to the candidates and their managers what they consider to be objectionable rhetoric.

It is only natural to ask why the need to append all these petty human foibles, to which almost no one is immune, to the awesome Sinaitic commandments? The Talmud reminds us that "many are guilty of robbery, a minority is guilty of lewdness, but all are guilty of slander." Did the Sages have a deliberate purpose in attaching the routine infractions, such as careless speech, to a major violation—giving false testimony or hiring someone to testify in your favor? The answer may not be obvious, but it would appear that the Sages were fully committed to the thought that genuine belief in God was not to be found primarily in noble pronouncements delivered from the mountaintop but rather in the way one chooses to order his/her life down below—at home, in the neighborhood and in the marketplace. The much-repeated aphorism that God is found in the details is what occupied the concern of the eminent authorities.

A basic moral problem is that telling a little lie is not regarded as a serious infraction by most people. It is not in the same category as stealing or destroying another's property, both of which are seen as major violations. Lying, on the other hand, seems trivial, a temporary lapse that is almost expected of normal people as a self-defensive measure. If you are testifying in court under oath, you are expected to tell the truth, "so help me God," but, outside the court, God is not expected to care that much if you deviate from the straight and narrow path. God has more important matters to deal with than to be concerned with little lies and half-truths.

Some of our most venerable religious authorities, however, view truth telling with utmost seriousness, comparable to the other major commandments. "When will the Messiah arrive?" Reb Pinhas of Koretz asked. "When people will regard the utterance of a lie as sinful as adultery," the Rebbi concluded.

Abraham Joshua Heschel reminds us that in the Hebrew Bible there is no equation of God with any of His attributes, such as love, justice, or compassion. However, in Jewish liturgy (based on Jeremiah 10:10), the equation can be found: "God is Truth. Love, justice, compassion are merely expressions of the Divine, not its highest manifestation. Truth is always with God. It is the mystery of being. Therefore, the way that always leads to God is Truth" (*A Passion For Truth,* p.164).

Elsewhere in the same volume in which he analyzes the life and work of Rabbi Mendl of Kotzk, Heschel summarizes the thesis of his book: "The habit of lying is tantamount to lynching the soul. Yet people generally consider the utterance of a lie to be a triviality. . . throughout history mendacity has been the mother of cruelty, canards and deception, the prelude to murder and war. . ." (p.12)

Why do decent people choose to lie when they could take the simple route of consistently sticking to the truth? Lying is a very complex activity. It often takes intelligence to tell a convincing lie; lying also requires a keen memory so as not to contradict oneself. Lying requires effort and creativity. Yet, so many people prefer the escape route of lying rather than direct confrontation that truth-telling requires of us.

People choose to lie for different reasons. Some of us lie presumably to make others feel good, and who wants to resist a false compliment even when we know it is not really true?

Two Talmudic teachers debate this very situation regarding the physical appearance of a bride at her wedding. The school of Shammai says: "Describe the bride as she is." Without frills; without falsehood. The school of Hillel says: "Describe the bride as beautiful and graceful." The school of Shammai retorted to the school of Hillel: "But suppose she is lame or blind. Is one to say, 'O bride, so lovely and graceful,' seeing that Scripture declares, 'Keep far from a false word'" (Ex.23:7)? The school of Hillel replied to the school of Shammai: "In your opinion, if a person has made a bad purchase in the marketplace, should his friend praise it to his face or belittle it? Surely he should praise it to his face." Hence, the Sages inferred that an individual should always try to be pleasant to other people (B.Ketubot 16b).

Hillel certainly understood the implication of what he was saying: it is worthwhile to depart slightly from the cold truth in order to raise another person's hopes or self-esteem. The problem with Hillel's generous view is that it may encourage the flatterer to exploit others by giving them an unrealistic picture of themselves.

We should also be reminded that in recent years some astute educators have warned parents and teachers not to heap more praise on a child than he/she deserves, especially when the child has not shown sufficient effort. When the child is made to feel that whatever the performance, he/she will be extravagantly praised, then the child may lose the motivation to improve and will probably detect the lack of honesty on the part of the teacher or parent. Exaggerated praise, especially when it is not justified, can be almost as damaging as the absence of praise when it is deserved.

Others resort to lying in order to make *themselves* feel good or to raise their own self- esteem. The need to shield themselves from criticism propels them to lie. Although this need is frequently associated with children's behavior in order to avoid punishment, it is by no means restricted to young people. Chronic gamblers or alcoholics often lie to a family member or to an employer about their self-destructive pattern so as to maintain their reputation as responsible people. Others, even without such chronic problems, nevertheless resort to lying in order to gain the needed approval of people whom they wish to impress.

Although the need to lie to another person, whether friend or stranger, reveals a significant character flaw, a distinction should be made between the chronic liar who cannot be believed even when he tells the truth, and the person who on a rare occasion may deviate from the truth in order to save his own or another's reputation, or in the special treatment of a bride on her wedding day.

I recall being asked to give a reference for an employee of our synagogue whose contract was not renewed by our board of directors. Although no one questioned his integrity, he lacked the expertise that the synagogue required of him. I could not bring myself to spoil his chance to obtain another job in synagogue administration. I wrote a positive reference on his behalf without indicating why he was denied a new contract. My letter could be construed as failure on my part to reveal the whole truth, but after much deliberation I concluded that the employee had to support a young, growing family. Furthermore, I rationalized that another congregation, perhaps smaller than ours, would probably be less demanding of him and would appreciate his warm personality in addition to his other skills which could serve him well. I did not feel pangs of guilt for arriving at my decision. Yet, I was fully aware that my lack of full disclosure could be regarded as a falsehood, or a form of *genevat da-at*, especially if he failed to be productive in his new position.

Some individuals are careful not to lie in the presence of others, yet they have trouble telling themselves the truth. For want of a better term, we often refer to their evasion as denial. (Many of us have undoubtedly seen the clever bumper sticker: "Denial is not only a river in Egypt"). Denial usually affects the denier more than those associated with him, yet people close to the denier cannot help but become affected by a lack of candor. The denier seems unable or unwilling to confront his physical or emotional problems. For example, a person has been coping with pain for a protracted period, yet, he cannot face the real possibility that something could be seriously wrong.

Another case of denial: A couple has been experiencing serious marital problems. One partner insists on seeking professional help; the other partner doesn't want to recognize that the marriage is unraveling or that he/she may be at least partially to blame. The denier is either obtuse or unprepared to confront the stark reality of a relationship in trouble. The denier conveniently lies to him/herself, hoping that the problem will correct itself and disappear, if it is even a problem at all.

Consider the case of parents who have been told by their son's teachers that he has become a serious discipline problem in class. The parent does not choose to face reality, and prefers to blame the teachers for their impatience or incompetence. No one benefits from the "cover up," least of all the difficult child to whom attention must be paid.

Lying to oneself does not carry the same moral stigma as lying to one's friends or co-workers. It appears to be more an emotional than a moral disorder, and yet self-deception may be hurtful to others, family or friends, who are adversely affected by the denier's unwillingness to be candid with himself.

Lying comes in an infinite variety of guises and masks. We can never measure the full effect of a lie. But it always exacts a price and, most harmful of all, it pollutes the environment by creating a climate of skepticism and distrust.

I have long pondered over the meaning of the Midrash that reveals that "Everything in the world was created by God except the art of lying." It is apparent that the author of this profound insight wishes to emphasize that God is the Creator of everything, both good and evil, that we find in our world. The prophet Isaiah exclaims that the one God creates both good and evil. God is responsible for both life and death. Even the natural deterioration of the body in the form of disease and illness—often a prelude to death—may be attributed to God's plan. But lying is a voluntary, personal act for which the fabricator alone is responsible. God establishes an unbridgeable distance between Himself and the liar, who alone must bear the consequences for subverting the truth. No matter how brilliant or creative the lie, the creator of a deliberate and harmful falsehood has alienated himself from the Creator.

I have often wondered whether the great Hasidic rabbi, Levi Yitzhak of Berdichev, was teaching his disciples that truth-telling was more important than Sabbath observance or that no Jew, even the heretic, is without some merit.

On his way to the synagogue on the Sabbath, Levi Yitzhak confronts a young man who lights up a cigarette in the rabbi's presence. The rabbi reminds him that this is the holy Sabbath.

"I haven't forgotten that," answers the young man.

"Do you not know the law prohibiting us to smoke on Shabbos?"

"Yes, I know the law," the young man replies.

Levi Yitzhak looks toward heaven and addresses the Holy One: "Did you hear his response?" he asks. "True, this young man is desecrating the Shabbos, but notice that nothing will cause him to tell a lie."

It appears to this observer that the hasidic sage held fast to both virtues—truth-telling and compassion for his people. He would embrace all Jews excepting those who would not stand up to the truth.

# Insights From The Sages

## Hiding the Truth Is Equated with Idolatry

Rabbi Eleazar said: "He who conceals the truth in his speech is as one who worships idols, for Jacob [disguised as Esau] said of himself, 'I will be in his eyes as one who makes a *mockery* of him' (Gen. 27:12), and with regard to idols it is said, 'They are a delusion, a work of *mockery*'" (Jer. 10:15).

(B. Sanhedrin 92a)

## Who Are Disqualified Witnesses?

And these are ineligible [to be witnesses or judges since their word cannot be relied upon]: A gambler with dice, a usurer, a trainer of pigeons, and traffickers in Sabbatical year produce... Rabbi Judah said: "When is this the case? If this is their sole occupation. But if they have other means of livelihood, they are eligible."

(Mishnah Sanhedrin Ch. 3)

## God Created Everything but Falsehood

Rabbi Samuel ben Nahman says: We find that the Holy One created everything in His world; only the qualities of falsehood and exaggeration were not His doing. Mortals devised false words out of their own hearts, as it is said, "Conceiving and uttering from their own hearts words of falsehood" (Is. 59:13).

(Pesikta Rabbati [Yale J. S.] p. 509)

## The Deceiver Is Deceived

When Jacob discovered that his bride was Leah, he angrily exclaimed: "You deceiver, and daughter of a deceiver!" Leah responded: "Is there a teacher without pupils? Did your father not call you 'Esau' and you responded to him! So, when you called me [Rachel] I answered you."

(Beresheet Rabbah 70)

לֹא תַחְמֹד בֵּית רֵעֶךָ
לֹא תַחְמֹד אֵשֶׁת רֵעֶךָ
וְעַבְדּוֹ וַאֲמָתוֹ וְשׁוֹרוֹ
וַחֲמֹרוֹ וְכֹל אֲשֶׁר לְרֵעֶךָ.

You shall not covet your
neighbor's house;
you shall not covet your
neighbor's wife, or his male
or femal slave, or his ox
or his ass, or anything that is
your neighbor's.

# Tenth Commandment

# Reflections

It was only in recent years that I discovered that the first and last commandments were closely related, following a symmetrical pattern. Unlike the other eight commandments dealing with action—both positive and negative— the opening and final commandments are concerned with an attitude, a way of thinking about God and one's fellow human beings. Once we accept the existence of a personal God and we make a serious effort not to envy that which rightfully belongs to another person, then we can reasonably move from attitude to action: you shall not steal, commit adultery, etc. The appropriate thoughts concerning God and the person next door sets the tone for observing the other commandments requiring action. We may think of the first and tenth commandment as "bookends" which enclose and validate the other commandments.

The concluding commandment seems clear until the reader begins to delve into the meaning of the key words in the text. 1. What does the Hebrew word for covet, *hamod*, really imply? 2. Does the expression *lo titaveh*, "you shall not crave," found in the second version of the Decalogue (Deuteronomy 5:18), mean the same as "you shall not covet" or does it convey a different meaning? 3) Is there a deliberate pattern or order found in the tenth commandment? 4) Does the Torah imply that it is possible for humans to eliminate feelings of envy from their lives? If so, what happens to that pervasive drive for acquiring material things, for improving one's finan-

cial status? Is the acquisitive drive that is encouraged in a capitalist society and the admonition against envy found in the
tenth commandment, irreconcilable?

1) The classical commentators are divided on the real meaning of the Hebrew expression, *lo tahmod*, "You shall not covet." A minority is of the opinion that the words are meant to
warn us against the destructive feelings of envy or acquisitive-
ness. The majority of commentators, however, disagree with
the contention that the biblical prohibition *lo tahmod* deals only
with an abstract feeling; they believe that it is rather an attitude accompanied by a deliberate plan or scheme to take possession of a person, animal or object for oneself. Even if one
forcibly persuades the owner of a desired object to sell it to
him, he is violating the commandment against coveting. The
majority view appears more reasonable because the commandment not to covet always focuses upon a specific object of
desire, the sight of which stimulates the craving to possess it
(Nahum Sarna, JPS commentary on Exodus, p. 114), whereas
the minority view would discourage ambition and its power to
contribute to society.

2) As for the double command found in Deuteronomy 5:18,
*you shall not covet* and *you shall not crave*, some scholars
contend that the second, unlike the first prohibition, addresses
the *feeling* of envy or jealousy which may be curbed by inner
discipline. Others comment that the two commands are synonymous; you cannot legislate a feeling or attitude. All depends on the way a person deals with his envy or greed, not
the feeling itself.

3) Is there a deliberate order found in the tenth commandment? In the version found in Deuteronomy, we are able to
detect a clear pattern, consisting of a descending order of importance: "You shall not covet your neighbor's wife. You shall
not crave your neighbor's house(household), or his field, or his
male or female slave, or his ox, or his ass, or anything that is
your neighbor's." We should also take note that "field" is found
only in the text found in Deuteronomy, and not in Exodus. When
the Decalogue was originally presented to the people of Israel,
they were a nomadic community. When the Book of Deuter-

onomy was written, most probably in a later period, the people had already settled in their land. Their status as landowners is reflected in the second version of the Decalogue.

4) Does the biblical tradition imply that it is possible to live without envy or jealousy? Since there is no punishment exacted for the feeling of envy, unless the dissatisfied person performs a harmful act in response to his feeling, we may assume that the Torah recognizes and accepts the pervasiveness of jealousy. Similarly, when the Torah declares, "You shall not hate your brother in your heart," it is meant as a cautionary note, an internal alarm that is sounded so that a person will not follow through on his feeling of hatred. The feelings of covetousness or hatred in themselves cannot be totally eradicated. They can be channelled in a more constructive direction, they may even be sublimated but not radically eliminated.

One of the guiding principles of Buddhism addresses this very problem. The root cause of unhappiness, the Buddha claims, is desire. The ills of life all flow from the passion for material pleasures, sex, success, the lust for power. By giving up all desire one can then attain the ideal of truth and inner peace. The vow of poverty and the renunciation of material needs is also practiced among certain Catholic orders. One may find a similar emphasis on the renunciation of desire among a small number of Jewish pietists and mystics, especially in the Middle Ages.

Although the Hasidic movement, which began in the eighteenth century, emphasized the necessity for joy and optimism, it also embraced another, more sober doctrine called *bittul hayesh*, "the annihilation of selfhood;" one must empty himself, so to speak, in order that he may achieve a sense of unity with God and be the recipient of His blessings.

But the extreme view of practicing voluntary self-denial never found popular acceptance in the Jewish mainstream, even among many pious Hasidim. Most Jews never regarded poverty as a desirable goal. On the contrary, poverty and dependence on others for one's basic needs was nothing less than a misfortune. The Grace After Meals contains the following prayer: "May we never find ourselves in need of gifts or loans from others, but may we rely upon Your helping hand, which is open, ample, and generous; thus we shall never suffer shame or humiliation" (*Siddur Sim Shalom for Weekdays*, p. 232). A moving prayer for self-support, *parnassah*, may be found in many traditional prayer books. In fact, prayers for material prosperity are found in the Jewish liturgy on the most spiritual holy day of the year when self-denial is required—the Yom Kippur fast.

How then may we seek to improve our financial status without feeling some sense of dissatisfaction with what we have thus far accumulated? Can we desire to purchase a more comfortable home for our own family without feeling some envy toward a more successful neighbor who has shown us his recent acquisition? Put another way, can one feel at home within a capitalist society without yearning for what others have? Is the admonition against coveting incompatible with the desire to climb the ladder of financial success?

Rabbi Samuel bar Nahman, one of the most renowned Palestinian scholars of the late third and early fourth centuries, understood the need for the aggressive drive in humans. He asked: How can the *yetzer ha-rah*, the aggressive impulse, be termed "very good?" Because Scripture teaches that were it not for the aggressive impulse, a man would not build a house, take a wife , beget children, or engage in commerce. All such activities come, as Solomon noted, from men's envy of one another (Genesis Rabbah 9:7).

There is little question that dissatisfaction with the status quo is the "machine" that drives the economy to greater heights. It is difficult to convince even an honest and benevolent entrepreneur that he should honor the tenth commandment when his growing enterprise thrives on wanting more than he presently has. The successful businessman is intent on building a bigger and better mousetrap than his competitor; even if he is able to squeeze him out of business, he will probably not be assailed by the business community as long as he remains within legal bounds. Is the commandment against covetousness just a pious anachronism that success-oriented men and women are not expected to take too seriously?

At the risk of appearing unrealistic, there is a way to recognize one's acquisitive nature without exploiting the person who has what we would like to possess. We should attempt to come to grips with the problem of needs vs. wants. How much do I realistically need to maintain myself and my family in a comfortable fashion without encroaching on another's possessions? If I am guided by my wants, I can never find enough to satisfy my insatiable hunger for more and more things. Envy of my neighbor's latest acquisition cannot help but affect our relationship. He cannot remain my loyal friend if I want what he has acquired. The only way that we can effectively deal with the problem of envy is to place a ceiling on our wants and to be guided by our needs, a fine distinction which requires honesty and candor with ourselves. Ben Zoma taught: "Who is rich? The person who is content with his portion" (Teachings of the Sages 4:1). Ben Zoma understood the relationship between needs and wants. Those who are able to make necessities their priority in place of their wants will have discovered genuine security and wealth.

What is so peculiar about covetousness or envy is that it is often irrational, unrelated to material deprivation. A person can afford to purchase a sports car no less expensive or eye-catching than the one his neighbor drives. Yet, envy of the neighbor's possession continues to consume him. Instead of finding a sense of satisfaction in "moving up" to his neighbor's status, he would prefer to see his neighbor fall on hard times and be forced to give up his expensive car.

Edgar Bronfman in *The Making of a Jew* relates a Russian story told to him by Seweryn Bialer. The story usually evokes a hearty laugh, but it is more serious than humorous for it poignantly reveals how irrational the envious person can become.

A Russian farmer was plowing his land and the blade struck a bottle. Out came a genie who offered him any wish in the world. The farmer had to explain his problem first. "Well, you see this farm. It is pretty poor, and not much grain grows in my field. You see my cow, how thin it is, and how it doesn't give much milk. My wife is fat, and the house is always filthy, and my children are practically juvenile delinquents. Ten kilometers to the west, I have a neighbor. He has a farm the size of mine. But the soil is so rich. His cow is fat and gives plenty of milk. His wife is beautiful and keeps a marvelous house; his children do well in school and are always neat and polite."

"Yes," said the genie, "and so?"

"My wish is," said the farmer, "that you make him like me!"

To speak of becoming *consumed* by envy is an appropriate metaphor. Obsessive envy is comparable to an illness which has the power to weaken one's physical and mental health. Envy can develop into a self-destructive illness.

Can the envious person be reached? It has been suggested that prayer can serve as an antidote to envy. A moving meditation found in the new Conservative *Siddur Sim Shalom* commences with the words: "May it be Your will, Adonai, my God and God of my ancestors, that envy of another not consume me, and that I will cause no one to become envious of me. . ." (Sabbath and Festival Prayer Book, p. 291).

Prayer may help as an effective antidote to the problem of envy, provided that the worshiper feels the need to re-arrange his priorities. God does not respond to a personal prayer unless there is readiness by the worshiper to invite divine intervention.

The celebrated dramatist, novelist and poet Johann Wolfgang von Goethe also searched into the problem of envy and suggested a way to combat it. He concluded that "there is no remedy but love." But how can a person blinded by envy, which is not far-removed from outright hostility, replace one passion by another? The oft-quoted prescription proclaimed by Jesus to love your enemy is psychologically difficult, if not impossible to attain. The Hebrew Bible speaks of the need to help one's enemy and the Talmud expresses the spiritual value of converting an enemy into a friend.

Willard Gaylin, a prominent psychoanalyst and ethicist, observes that the only true antagonist of envy is *identification*, the fusion of fate and feeling. "As envy separates us from our fellows, identification joins them to us. . . My friends' victories are my victories as are his joys and sadnesses. . . Identification binds us to others in a common fate. It permits for compassion, sympathy and empathy" (*Feelings,* Harper and Rowe, p. 147).

The ability to identify with the person who has successfully accumulated more than ourselves may not automatically eliminate envy and covetousness, but it may offer a viable alternative to negative feelings toward that person. He is no longer regarded as an opponent, an adversary, but someone deserving of what he has, and thus, entitled to my respect.

Like most people, I have found myself struggling with the agonizing feeling of envy. I personally have experimented with the following two steps:

a) *Introspection.* I ask the question, "why must I permit the feeling of envy to take control? What does it matter in the scheme of things if I earn less than a colleague or have fewer possessions than another professional living in my neighborhood?" I have never had to struggle against deprivation. I have also trained myself to rely on some of the intangibles that money cannot buy in order to achieve genuine security and comfort.

b) *Practice what I preach.* I have always attempted to teach my children and students that I am in no way superior to the next person—a basic religious value. The second part of the equation, however, is no less essential: *Neither is the other person superior to me.* I have no valid reason to envy him, just as he has no need to envy me. We can admire each other's skills and accomplishments without permitting feelings of jealousy to alienate each other. If my neighbor and I enjoy genuine equality, we should be able to respect our differences in natural endowment or economic status without permitting envy to damage our relationship.

Usually we find that envy and covetousness carry negative connotations in the Jewish tradition. "Jealousy, lust and ambition expel a man from the world" (Pirkei Avot 4:21); "Jealousy is as cruel as the grave"(Song of Songs 8:6). However, the Sages also note the positive side of envy and covetousness. The following rabbinic aphorism is most revealing: *Kinat sof-*

*erim tarbeh hokhma,* when scholars are envious of each other, wisdom is increased. The author apparently acknowledged that envy was a natural human trait, but if it were shifted from the materialistic to the academic or intellectual realm, then the competitive spirit—even if based on envy—could help advance knowledge and wisdom. Such rivalry could prove a blessing. Although the original meaning of the rabbinic proverb was directed exclusively to healthy competition among students of Torah, it may also be applied to the keen competitive spirit in the area of modern science where the drive to find cures for human ailments, both physical and psychological, has created remarkable results in recent years.

Abraham Joshua Heschel in his inspirational book, *The Sabbath,* finds an ennobling meaning to the tenth commandment, *You shall not covet.* In the Sabbath liturgy we recite: "You were pleased with the seventh day and sanctified it, the most coveted of days did You call it." Heschel asks: Where in the Bible is the Sabbath called "the most coveted of days"? The verse in Genesis 2:2, which we usually translate: "and God completed on the seventh day," is rendered in an ancient Aramaic version: "and God coveted the seventh day."

Heschel continues: "Do not covet anything belonging to thy neighbor; I have given thee something that belongs to Me. What is that something? A day." The Sabbath seeks to replace the coveting of things in space with coveting events that occur in time, teaching us to covet the seventh day all the days of the week. God coveted that day, calling it *hemdat yamim,* a day to be coveted. "It is as if the command: *Do not covet things of space,* were correlated with the unspoken word: *Do covet things of time*" (pp. 90, 91).

# Insights from the Sages

## To Covet Is to Carry out Desire

A situation in which you want his daughter for your son, or his son for your daughter is excluded [from covetousness]. Perhaps the mere verbal expression on one's desire for a neighbor's things is also meant? But it says: "You shall not covet the silver or gold that is on them and take it for yourself" (Deut. 7:25). Just as there [in that command] only the carrying out of one's desire into practice is forbidden, so also here [in all other cases] it is forbidden only to carry out the desire into practice.

(Mekhilta Ba-hodesh 8)

## Finding Contentment with One's Lot

"Honor the Lord with whatever excellence He has bestowed upon you" (interpretation of Prov. 3:9).If you are a handsome person, do not go astray after lewdness, but honor your Creator, and revere Him, and praise Him for the good looks He has bestowed upon you.

(Pesikta Rabbati (Yale J.S.) pg 516)

## We Wish Only the Best for a Child and Pupil

Rabbi Joseph bar Honi said: A man envies everyone except his son and his disciple. One's son, as shown by the example of Solomon (David's son); and one's disciple, as shown by Elisha's saying to Elijah, "I pray you, let a double portion of your spirit be upon me" (II Kings 2:9); or if you prefer, Moses' giving of his spirit to Joshua: "He laid his hands upon him, and commissioned him" (Num. 27:23).

(B. Sanhedrin 105b)

# Afterword

Friends are curious to hear what motivates an author to write a particular book. Most of the books I have been privileged to write were developed from courses given to teenagers or adults. This volume as well was initially inspired in the classroom of the Fair Lawn Jewish Center where I taught adult classes for forty-one years.

While cleaning out my bulging filing cabinet before retiring from the active rabbinate, I accidentally came across an outline for a ten-week course on rediscovering the meaning of the Ten Commandments and how they apply to our daily lives. After each Tuesday's class was over, I also jotted down summaries of our lively discussions in the classroom.

Before the semester was completed I requested each student to write what he/she would personally add as an eleventh commandment, if given the choice. I asked them, "What essential lesson would you want to leave to posterity if you were empowered to be heard and quoted for generations to come?"

Most students expressed a sense of reluctance to add anything to this immortal document which has withstood the test of time, and is still revered by much of the civilized world, even though inconsistently followed. Yet, after revealing some apprehension, they seemed ready to try their hand at expressing what they would regard as a guiding moral principle, perhaps worthy of being added to the "Big Ten." Some of their responses created an indelible impression on me. Here is a sampling of their contributions:

"*You shall use your* sekhel *(common sense) along with the commandments.* It is not enough to go through the motions of observing the Ten Commandments just because they were set down in the sacred Torah. Maturity demands that we learn to apply each commandment for the proper occasion and under the right circumstances. Without *sekhel* an appropriate choice may be made, but for the wrong reason. For example, I know someone who will not openly disagree with his aging father primarily because he doesn't want to lose his portion of the inheritance. If the son had more *sekhel*, he would have shared more time with his parents when they were seeking a relationship with him."

"*You shall not become a fanatic.* We have personally seen too many good people hurt by fanatical parents or other rigid authority figures. Each religious group has the right to establish moral standards and requirements such as we find in the Decalogue, but in a free society such as ours no authority may demand compliance from others unless we flagrantly violate the laws or statutes of our land. In a voluntary religious community such as ours, more people who are victimized by authoritarian personalities leave the fold than those attracted to the religious life. They are repelled by the grip of the religious fanatic."

"*You shall not become self-righteous.* I admire the people around me who strive to live by the principles found in the Decalogue. I try to live by these principles as well. But I fume when I see people look down on those who fail to live up to *their* moral standards. They constantly preach to others as if there is only one right way, and they are certain they have discovered God's secret. Only they are in the know. A genuinely religious person will not call himself religious or righteous. He should leave that to others."

The only student who came up with a cynical reply blurted out, "*Thou shalt not get caught!*" Naturally, he drew laughter from the rest of the class, which I initially felt, was the purpose of his disturbing response. My facial expression registered my sense of surprise, knowing him to be a person of proven integrity and above-average intelligence.

After reading his written statement before the class, I grew less hostile toward my provocative student, although I vehemently rejected his reasoning, as did most of the class. He wrote: "I have never been a revolutionary or an anarchist, yet, I have resented spending too much of my childhood and adulthood being told what I can and cannot do. I need to be free to decide for myself what is right and wrong, not to be handed down rules and laws intended to tame a generation of former slaves. So if I can just do as I please, rely on my own sense of right and wrong, and avoid being punished for what I do and don't do, then I will continue to be my own person and enjoy the freedom I deserve."

A friend of this person, responded from the back of the room with uncharacteristic passion: "People who agree to live in a lawful society and abide by reasonable moral laws, such as those found in the Ten Commandments, are really freer than those who must worry about being found out and apprehended. I would hate to live in fear of being caught and subsequently dragged into court. Who wants to live in constant fear of possibly ending up in jail?" I had the distinct feeling that the majority of the class was pleased with the reply of their spokesperson. I certainly was though I deliberately limited my verbal reactions so the students could have their say without interference from their teacher..

The class then turned to me. They had every right to ask the same question of me that I posed to them. What contribution would I make to the heated discussion? I confessed that I needed more time to think about the question than my students since my orientation was different than theirs. Weren't the "Ten Utterances," as they are called in the Torah, revealed at Mount Sinai? So was I was taught to believe, and so have I continued to believe throughout my life despite brief periods of skepticism. Would it not be audacious, if not sacrilegious, to add another commandment of my own! Doesn't the Book of Deuteronomy proclaim explicitly, "You shall not add anything to what I command you or take anything away from it, but keep the commandments of the Lord your God that I enjoin upon you" (4:2)?

In the final analysis, I had little choice but to participate in my own little quiz; I could not be like a basketball coach standing on the sideline. I was forced to enter the game with the other players. However, instead of offering an additional commandment, I suggested a *klal gadol*, an essential principle, which I believed was worthy of inclusion along with the basic commandments. Rather than coming up with an original addition to the Ten Commandments, I relied on the superlative charge that Hillel gave to a prospective convert who wanted the whole Torah summarized for him while on the run, or as the text expresses it, while standing on one leg. And Hillel's patient response: "That which is hateful to you, do not do to your neighbor." I could not find a more appropriate guiding principle than this.

A perceptive woman in the class, herself a convert to Judaism, wanted to know why, if I was not going to offer something original, would I not choose the direct and positive command found in Leviticus (19:18), "And you shall love your neighbor as yourself." She also remembered from her private classes with me that the preeminent scholar Rabbi Akiba called this verse from Leviticus *klal gadol ba-Torah*, the great, or better, the embracing principle found in the Torah. And she was correct. Yet, I defended my personal choice before the class, contending that it is unrealistic to love another person as much as we love ourselves. To add another problem to the troublesome text, many of us do not know how to love ourselves properly, so how can we love our neighbor when we are so often deficient in feeling love of oneself? Because of the difficulty of properly fulfilling this biblical command, many efforts have been made to reinterpret the verse. One example: And you shall love your neighbor, for that person is like yourself, equal to you in worth.

Hillel's charge, however, can be clearly understood by most of us. We know what we do not like done to ourselves. Anything that is done to us which we find objectionable, whether a hateful word or a hurtful gesture, we must choose not do to another person, whether a family member, friend or stranger.

But why choose Hillel's principle as a "rider" to the Decalogue? It is possible to follow the commandments in a literal sense but still lose sight of what makes for a warm and sensitive relationship with others. How may we learn to avoid the temptation to hurt our parents even though we may be following the rules of what constitutes filial honor and respect? Hillel's admonition can be grasped by just about anyone: If you object to something that may be done to you, then avoid doing the same to the next person. Hillel brings the lofty commands in the Decalogue down to earth by providing a human framework for their implementation.

An older member of the class who attended with his daughter-in-law inquired whether Hillel was charging the disciple to be a *mensch* above all else. Yet another participant chimed in: "If Hillel would have been acquainted with Yiddish, he would probably have said just that to his inquiring student."

\* \* \*

Yehudah Amichai (1924-2000), perhaps Israel's most celebrated poet, fully deserves the last word on the discussion of adding to the original commandments. In his latest book of poems published shortly before his death, *Open Closed Open*, Amichai relates how his father lovingly impressed each of the commandments on him in his youth.

> Then he turned his face to me one last time,
> as on the day he died in my arms, and said, I
> would like to add two more commandments: the
> Eleventh Commandment, "Thou shalt not change,"
> and the Twelfth Commandment, "Thou shalt
> change. You will change." Thus spoke my
> father, and he walked away and disappeared
> into his strange distances.

Amichai's two additional commandments can only be understood when joined together as one unit. *Thou shalt not change*: You should not feel the need to outgrow this awesome moral code merely because your personal circumstances may have changed. You have grown intellectually or you have become prosperous since your early years when you were taught these Ten Commandments. You may no longer feel the need to be burdened by these ancient moral directives.

*Thou shalt not change.* Do not regard these words as relative rules or suggestions that no longer apply to this complex contemporary world.

*Thou shalt change. You will change*: As vital as these commandments are to your moral life, you should not rely exclusively on them in their original form to answer all your current moral dilemmas. As times change, so do unanticipated moral problems require change within yourself so that you may learn to deal with the agonizing problems of our age. Though you do not outgrow the ethical laws delineated in the Decalogue, you must also be prepared to address the perplexing moral dilemmas that confront every succeeding generation.

Yehudah Amichai calls on us to change, to accept contemporary wisdom even as we tenaciously hold to the tried and tested words that have guided the chain of generations ever since the Revelation at Sinai.